A String of
EXPRESSION

Techniques for Transforming
Art and Life Into Jewelry

JUNE ROMAN

NORTH LIGHT BOOKS
Cincinnati Ohio

14 13 12 11 10   5 4 3 2 1

Distributed in Canada by Fraser Direct
100 Armstrong Avenue
Georgetown, ON, Canada L7G 5S4
Tel: (905) 877-4411

Distributed in the U.K. and Europe by David & Charles
Brunel House, Newton Abbot, Devon, TQ12 4PU, England
Tel: (+44) 1626 323200, Fax: (+44) 1626 323319
Email: postmaster@davidandcharles.co.uk

Distributed in Australia by Capricorn Link
P.O. Box 704, S. Windsor, NSW 2756 Australia
Tel: (02) 4577-3555

Library of Congress Cataloging-in-Publication Data

Roman, June.
    A string of expression / June Roman. -- 1st ed.
        p. cm.
    Includes bibliographical references and index.
    ISBN-13: 978-1-60061-791-1 (pbk. : alk. paper)
    ISBN-10: 1-60061-791-3 (pbk. : alk. paper)
    1. Jewelry making. I. Title.
    TT212.R65 2010
    739.27--dc22
                                2009040440e

www.fwmedia.com

Editor: Tonia Davenport
Cover Designer: Michelle Thompson
Interior Designer: Corrie Schaffeld
Production Coordinator: Greg Nock
Photographers: Christine Polomsky, Richard Deliantoni

ACKNOWLEDGEMENTS

Writing this book has been one of the most rewarding experiences of my life, even though there were moments when I thought it a bit overwhelming. The task of eloquently scripting the underpinnings of my soul onto the pages of a manuscript appeared daunting and could not have been accomplished without the unwavering support and encouragement from a host of family members, friends and the truly awesome North Light Team. I wish to bestow a most sincere and heartfelt thank-you to the following people:

- Andrea, my precious daughter, who stepped up to the plate and carried out numerous duties and responsibilities that were otherwise mine. I love you.

- Kathy, the best sister anyone could have, thanks for imparting intelligent feedback, supplying steadfast support and for persuading me to trust in my own abilities.

- My most treasured mother, who has always believed in me even when I did not believe in myself.

- Rema, a solid rock of encouragement, who granted much needed respites and was the recipient of endless phone conversations that went something like this:
  Rema: "How are you?"
  Me: "I'm going crazy."
  Rema: "Why are you going crazy?"
  Me: "Blah, blah, blah…"

- Cheryl, the first person who called me an artist.

- Debbie, a true friend who stayed up until the wee hours cutting and stitching small suede circles for my prototype experiments.

- My running buddies at work: Cindy, Pam, Heather, Katrina, Kim, Vallie and Debbie for providing encouragement, much needed humor and for always believing in my creative abilities. You are my most ardent cheerleaders!

- The North Light Team for doing what you do best in such a superior manner.

- Christine Polomsky, photographer extraordinaire, who transformed what initially appeared to be a terrifying experience into one of the best times of my life.

- Tonia Davenport, my superb editor and guiding light, thank you from the bottom of my heart for making the decision to take a chance on a relatively unknown "raw" artist with a crazy idea for a book. Your belief in me and my vision for this book are none other than priceless. I will be forever grateful.

THANK YOU.

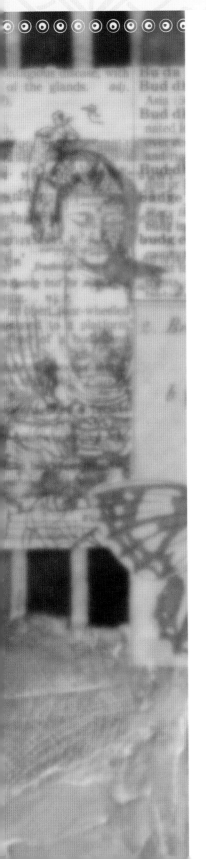

CONTENTS

THE ROOTS OF AUTHENTIC DESIGN 6

DRAWING INSPIRATION FROM LIFE 8

BASIC TOOLS AND SUPPLIES 10

NATURE'S RENDERINGS 12
BLISS 14
SPRING 18
TREE 22
AUTUMN 30
ORGANIC ELEMENTS 34

A SENSE OF PLACE 38
HOME 40
SKY 46
SECRET 52
WABI-SABI 56

LIFE 62
LAYERS 64
HEALING BUDDHA 68
EMPTY NEST 76
WEDDING DAY 80

CULTURAL CONSCIOUSNESS 84
AFRICAN WOMAN 86
TIBETAN 92
ABORIGINAL 98
LANTERN 102

COLOR EXPLORATION 106
INDIGO 108
TWO SIDES 114
SUNSET 120

RESOURCES 124

INDEX 125

ABOUT JUNE 127

All true artists, whether they know it or not, create from a place of no-mind, from inner stillness.
—*Eckhart Tolle*

THE ROOTS OF AUTHENTIC DESIGN

The only time I feel perfect is when I am creating, transforming, designing something—anything. As a very young child I had unlimited imaginative powers. I possessed the ability to shape an idea into a blueprint for happiness; it was like magic. At some point, this ability began to diminish and, in time, became more difficult to conjure up. I would venture inside art stores, explore the aisles for hours and depart empty-handed. At some future point, I would return, purchase a delicious caché of art supplies and wait for inspiration to commence. It never did. Once, I even bought a wooden drawing table, to which I attached a bright-yellow metallic lamp that swiveled in every direction; but alas, I never drew anything on my drawing board. I spent years in this artless funk. It wasn't until I discovered jewelry design (thanks to my sister), and subsequently art journaling, that I became enthralled with the prospect of joining the creative portion of the human race once again.

I had stumbled upon my muse—who was indeed a flirt—and enjoyed playing with beads, resin, clay, paint, crayons, glue, decorative papers and a host of other elements. In a sense, I was reborn—prepared now to wield the powerful tools of creativity yet again; I had uncovered a way to express my artistic voice.

What does art journaling have to do with jewelry design? There are two possible answers: nothing at all or absolutely everything! Let's suppose the latter is the case. After I complete an art journal page, a mental process begins to transpire. I may be moved by the colors, the images may evoke an onslaught of feelings and the text may serve as a springboard for ideas. This collective chain of events is occurring simultaneously, and, if I allow myself to surrender during this process, inspiration becomes its natural by-product. Designs for some of the most dynamic and unique jewelry pieces begin to emerge. Pieces created out of this authentic mindset hold immense meaning and depth because the truest part of me is embedded within their layers. Anyone following this paradigm can have the same incredible results, especially if you are the kind of person who enjoys expressing your artistic vision through more than one medium.

I love the process of working on a jewelry piece one day and a mixed-media page the next, particularly since my attention span is rather short. This made it necessary to install two large work areas in my spare room, which eventually became my studio. One space is dedicated to art journaling while the other holds all of the materials/equipment needed for beading and jewelry design. It wasn't long before I developed my own signature style. I was on fire. The flames of inspiration gave birth to an online jewelry store, a blog, brand new photography skills and the opportunity to be published. I am grateful and blessed that I am able to live and flourish artfully.

Since I had spent so much time in an artistic depression, I began contemplating the process of inspiration. Where does it come from? Why are some people able to access it more easily than others? What happens when it dies and how can it be revived? Is it possible to remain continually inspired? Can one actually document the illusive process of creativity? That is when I started taking a serious look at how I developed ideas for my pieces. Did they come out of thin air? Not really. Often I am inspired by nature, trips to museums, films, photographs, dreams, poetry and music. However, the realization that an art journal page was the basis for many of my quirky designs was definitely my "aha" moment. I decided to pay attention. Combining my love for jewelry design and art journaling was beginning to sound a lot like a blueprint for happiness.

Are you ready to break out and do something entirely new? Are you having difficulty discerning exactly what your creative muse is saying? Sharing techniques on how to transform life and art into striking and original pieces of jewelry is my dream for you. My intention is that this book serves as an artistic booster shot for jewelry artists who wish to explore the boundless realm of creativity and take their design skills to another level.

I have a promiscuous muse. My muse wants to own every color, work in many media, and in numerous genre.
—*Mary Klotz*

DRAWING INSPIRATION FROM LIFE

The innocence of childhood, followed by years of living dangerously, building a career, marriage, the birth of a child, divorce, new beginnings . . . this is the stuff of life. These are the experiences that influence us, shape us and, at times, can even break us. We all have our stories to tell. Some we broadcast to anyone who will listen, others are tucked securely away in the deep recesses of our heart and the rest are buried within the infinitesimal bits of our soul—surfacing on that rare occasion when we are strong enough to stand alone before the mirror and face our own truth, and then . . . just like that, we are set free.

I have found that art journaling is a perfect way for me to pour out my emotions on paper. I notice that my continual mind "chatter" ceases. I move fearlessly through this process taking risks with paint, tearing paper, cutting out text and gluing images until I am tired and satisfied. When I look closer with an analytical eye, I may discover a repetitive archetype, a metaphorical image or an underlying message from the subconscious. This information goes a long way in helping me to see myself with new eyes.

Art journaling is a way of keeping a soul diary. These visual images possess color, shape, texture, design, emotions and truth. This layered landscape can become your mood board from which to draw limitless ideas and points of inspiration. Designers often use mood boards to visually project the style or feel they wish to convey in a particular project. Drawing stimulation from the deepest part of your being inevitably results in revolutionary design. How can you fail using this approach? It's impossible.

How do the images from our journals morph into jewelry? The same way a filmmaker turns a script into a movie or an interior decorator relies on her sketches to design a bedroom. Begin by visualizing how the dominant images/emotions from your art page correspond to a variety of materials. For example, the icy blue color of kyanite briolettes looks like water; shells lend texture and could also be a reminder of the sea; vintage patina copper beads may symbolize a zen-like peacefulness; and darkened sterling silver coupled with crystal emanates romance. A medium such as Precious Metal Clay offers us the freedom to mold or stamp any image we desire in an effort to accomplish our design goals. Incorporating text, photos and other images within a bezel and resin imparts the opportunity to pull phrases and words directly from the pages of our journals. Hopefully this book will offer you a range of techniques to make your jewelry designs a reality.

A jewelry piece should be an aesthetically pleasing arrangement of color, shape, texture and design. Pull all of the aforementioned from your art pages and you will have a successful formula for an original piece of jewelry. Although I have included a list of materials for each of the projects in this book, these materials reflect me and my personal expression. My ultimate desire is for you to go beyond my recipes and stretch the limits of your imagination to express your own stories. Remember, you are your muse. Determine how to capture the infinitesimal bits of your soul and transfigure them into something rare and beautiful—a unique expression of you.

Buy the best tools that you can afford—you will not regret it. Good tools really do perform better and make it easier for you to execute techniques.

TOOLS

Bent chain-nose pliers: These work in places that are difficult to reach and are great for pushing/squeezing the very tip of a wrapped wire close to the base for a neat appearance.

Chain-nose pliers: Use these for bending, pulling, holding, wrapping and shaping wire. Their jaws are not serrated, so they won't mar the wire.

Flat-nose pliers: I prefer these for bending wire at a 90-degree angle.

Round-nose pliers: These pliers form loops to make charms, connectors and jump rings. They are tapered so you can create loops in a variety of sizes.

Crimping pliers: Used with crimp beads or crimp tubes, a basic crimper forms a finished crimp bead whose diameter is less than 2mm smaller than the original crimp. This type of crimper was used for all of the projects in this book.

Super crimping pliers: Crimps all sizes of crimp tubes and beads. It has large and small grooved openings for folding and one opening for rolling both large and small tubes and beads.

Bench block and ball-peen hammer: Use these to hammer and flatten wire.

Hole punch: One of these is handy in a ⅛" (3mm) size, to punch holes in paper or fabric when you will be using ⅛" (3mm) eyelets.

Eyelets: These are metal rings connected to a tubular shaft—usually made of brass or aluminum—which serve as reinforcement to a hole in fabric or paper.

Eyelet setter: Use to set eyelets in fabric or paper by splaying and flattening the shaft.

Flush cutters: These trim wire close to the blades on the jaws of the pliers.

Diagonal flush cutters or wire cutters: These cutters are used to cut metal wire (such as silver and gold) as well as coated beading wire.

Bead clips: These handy clips are used to keep beads from slipping off stringing wire as you're working.

Velux (foam) mat: This provides a cushioned/textured surface on which to work and prevents beads from rolling around and onto the floor.

Beading boards/design layout boards: These are helpful, though not mandatory, for measuring necklace length, design and beading pattern preparation, and for bead placement.

MATERIALS

Coated stringing wire: I used Soft Flex Beading Wire Fine (.014 diameter, 21 strands) for all of the projects in this book.

Sterling silver wire (20- to 24-gauge): Used for wire-wrapping projects such as bead dangles, bead connectors, eye pins, etc.

Headpins: These are straight pieces of wire with a small head (which acts as a stopper) at the end, and they are used to make bead dangles or charms. I prefer those available in sterling silver.

Jump rings: Wire circles used to connect jewelry components. (The projects in this book call for both open and closed sterling silver jump rings.)

Crimp tubes: These are used to secure stringing wire. (I used 2mm tubes for all of the projects in this book.)

Crimp covers: These cover a crimp tube for a neater appearance; once covered it looks like a silver bead. I use a 4mm cover for a 2mm crimp tube.

Clasps: Used to connect the ends of necklaces and bracelets, these come in a wide range of styles. (I used the toggle or S-hook style for most of the closures in this book.)

PRECIOUS METAL CLAY (PMC) TOOL KIT

Precious Metal Clay (standard) or PMC+

Cutting mat: To protect the surface you are working on (especially if cutting with a craft knife).

Tile: Porcelain tile is an excellent surface on which to dry clay pieces.

Roller/PVC tube: Used to roll clay.

Ruler: To measure hole distances.

Craft knife: A very sharp knife, used to score/cut out clay pieces.

Filing tools: These will smooth the surface of your dry clay pieces.

Steel wool: Used to lift off tarnish from silver or to highlight patina surfaces.

Small coffee straws: These cut perfect holes in clay.

Clay smoothing tool: This smoothes out imperfections on wet clay.

Olive oil: I like to oil the surface of rubber stamps when using them with the clay, so that the clay releases easily.

Small plastic container with airtight lid and a damp sponge: This will keep the clay moist if you can't work with it for a bit after opening the package.

Liver of Sulfur (LOS): This is used to age or blacken silver, copper or brass. (I prefer the solid version.)

Steel brush: Use this to scrub and clean the white substance off clay pieces after they have been fired.

Assortment of rubber stamps or texturing mats: These are easy tools to use for adding texture, imagery or text to unfired clay.

Clay cutters: Available in a wide range of shapes and sizes—flowers, diamonds, triangles, etc. (I used the graduated circle clay cutters for the Healing Buddha necklace project [see page 68].)

Electric kiln: This is necessary to fire PMC pieces. If you do not own one, check to see where PMC classes are being taught in your area. Many places will fire your pieces for a nominal fee.

ART SUPPLIES

Watercolors

Golden's Crackle Paste

Golden's Gel Medium

Tim Holtz Distressed Ink Pad
(Tea Dye works great for me.)

Scissors

Paintbrushes

Golden's Fluid Acrylic Paint

Two-part doming resin, stirring sticks, plastic cups (I prefer and highly recommend ICE Resin. It dries crystal clear and is non-toxic [see Resources, page 124].)

Embroidery thread

Embroidery needles

Silk cord

MISCELLANEOUS

Text and pictures from old dictionaries or books

Dried flowers

Blank journal for jotting down design ideas

Ephemera

Tweezers

DREAM TOOLS

Oasis Concept Pads by Levenger: Each page has a blank section in the middle for drawing and ruled columns on the left and the right for writing notes, material lists, techniques and ideas. Wonderful to use for visual mapping and creating mood boards.

Kiln Paragon SC3: This is a great small jewelry kiln for the studio jeweler who works with silver, gold or bronze clay.

NATURE'S RENDERINGS

"My feet took a walk in the heavenly grass," is a lovely line from a poem written by Tennessee Williams. He understood the "tonic of the wilderness" that Henry Thoreau spoke of during his time at Walden Pond. Nature plays a strong role in many genres of art and jewelry design is no exception. Interpreting her language in our own work is essential. By doing so, we will expand the boundaries of our own creativity. Take advantage of what nature has to offer by experiencing its presence. Go for walks in the woods, stroll the beaches in contemplation, hike a trail or plant a garden. Coming in touch with nature is the same as coming in touch with ourselves.

Nature is just enough; but men and women must comprehend and accept her suggestions.
—Anne Wilson Schaef

Beyond the Universe Necklace
This variation, right, is inspired by the journal art on page 17; it is a variation on the Resin Collage technique (see page 16).

BLISS

Beyond the Universe

by June Roman

I am this rock eroded by harsh winds and trickling water
I am this hollow shell sheltering voices of the sea
I am this tree rocking to and fro, meditating purpose and bliss
I am this breeze, perfect in every way, reaching beyond the universe . . .

Artists frequently seek ways to express their spiritual experiences. Endeavoring to describe the unfathomable is, without question, quite difficult. Therefore, using the symbolic language of poetry serves as an excellent way to express such ethereal ideas. I attempted to do just that when I wrote the poem "Beyond the Universe," and the results were ripe for a mixed-media journal page which culminated in the creation of my delicate Bliss necklace.

It was a natural step to move from the poem to a mixed-media page. The poem conjures rich organic images of erosion and trickling water, as well as profound feelings of spiritual bliss and the act of deep meditation. Using the poem as my muse, I began by considering words such as sea, erosion and rock. These particular words influenced the textures I wished to create with materials such as crackle gesso paste, crumbled tissue paper and cheesecloth. The fertile, earthy color palette urged me to select mossy greens, azure blue, oxide yellow and burnt umber. Additionally, I wanted to include other natural elements such as leaves, pressed flowers (one of my favorite items; I frequently use them in my jewelry and mixed-media work), and images of nests, insects and old text.

Another great way to work with poetry is to choose words from a poem that begins with the same letter. These clever alliterations can be used as meaningful text for the future jewelry pieces. For example, the words bliss, breeze and beyond, stamped onto copper tags or precious metal clay, would make exquisite charms for a necklace or bracelet. Another idea would be to arrange selected text from the poem along with other natural elements in a bezel and suspend the arrangement in resin, as in the Bliss necklace. These "collage" bezels can serve as wonderful charms or pendants for necklaces.

The Bliss necklace seems to capture the essence of my art journal page which I entitled, Beyond the Universe. The dried flowers and text used in the bezel were directly lifted from the art journal page and poem. The collection of icy blue kyanite drops, faceted Chez glass and Nacazori pueblo beads depicts the trickling water. The copper pearls add a natural feel to the piece and the carved Asian design on the jade bead symbolizes meditation. The initial inspiration for the entire project stems from my original poetry. Moving from a poem to an art journal page to a necklace has unlimited possibilities! Follow where the inspiration leads, take a leap of faith and then . . . surrender.

This is love: to fly toward a secret sky, to cause a hundred veils to fall
each moment. First let go of life. Finally, to take a step without feet.

—Rumi

◎◎◎

MATERIALS

(Items in **bold** are needed for the stepped-out technique)

PENDANT

Bezel with rings, medium round bronze (Objects and Elements)

Portions of small dried flowers

Old dictionary text (bliss)

ICE Resin (Objects and Elements), including mixing cup and craft stick

Gel medium

Charm (copper pearl, bronze and copper spacers, headpin)

Oxidized jump ring, heavy large

Oxidized jump ring, medium

STRAND

Stringing wire

Crimps

Crimp covers

Copper pearls

Carved jade round

Bali bead cap

Copper bead

Sterling silver seed beads

Brown seed beads

Peruvian opal discs

Nacozari pueblo beads

Sterling silver spacers

Sterling silver rondelles

Sterling silver rounds

Oxidized sterling silver toggle clasp

Bronze spacers

HANGING CHARMS

Oxidized sterling silver small-link chain, 2' (61cm)

Oxidized head pins for bead charms

Kyanite drops

Small Nacozari pueblo beads

Peruvian discs

Small Chez glass rounds

TOOLS

Tweezers

RESIN COLLAGE

Suspending text, pictures and natural items within resin is a beautiful way to insert meaningful symbolism within any piece of jewelry. Sterling silver, bronze and copper bezels in various sizes can be purchased over the Internet (see Resources, page 124).

1. Seal a small dried flower with a bit of gel medium. Cut out tiny bits of text that you want to use. Glue the text and the flower into the back of the bezel, using small dots of gel medium and placing elements with a pair of tweezers.

2. To mix up the resin, first pour one measurement of the part A resin.

3. Pour in an equal amount of the part B hardener.

4. Fold the two parts together to mix, using a stir stick, until the resin is completely clear (about 2 minutes).

5. Pour the mixture into your bezel, or ladle it in, using your stick.

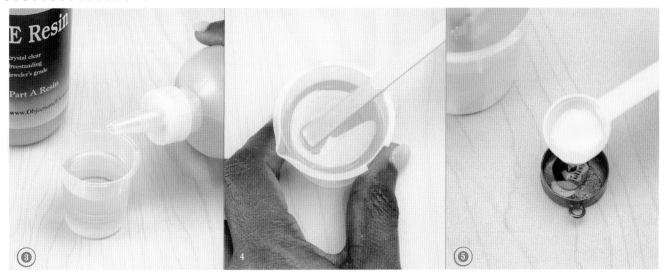

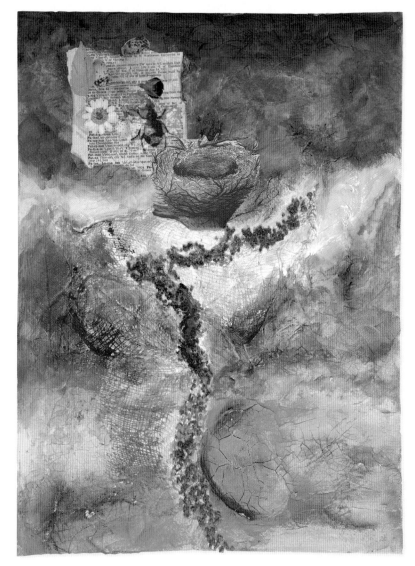

Beyond the Universe

An abstract representation of the "Beyond the Universe" poem. The earthy color palette and collage elements are infused nicely within the Bliss necklace.

SPRING

One way to begin a themed project is to repurpose your previous art pages by turning them into transparencies. The Spring art journal page is the result of an extension activity based on the Beyond the Universe art page (see page 17). In this example I have incorporated a transparency that I created after scanning Beyond the Universe and printing it out on transparency film. I printed out the Beyond the Universe poem onto transparency film as well, and attached it to the journal page with eyelets. Have fun experimenting with these transparent elements by placing unusual textures, papers, text and images under them, thereby creating more depth and interest.

Necklaces that have a centered focal point (a pendant or large bead) and mirror the same bead placement on either side of the midpoint are considered symmetrical. Straightforward, symmetrical design is easier to pull off and is generally successful. As you have gathered by now, I like the look of the unusual. I am naturally drawn to asymmetrical design and the use of eclectic materials. An asymmetrical composition still requires balance which makes this option a little tricky. It often requires more practice and some trial and error; however, this prototype offers more of a "wow" factor and encourages the artist to be more experimental.

In the Spring necklace, even though the opposite sides of the focal point do not mimic each other, there are commonalities. For example, the yellow jade rondelles echo the shape and color of the glass discs. Some of the same beads (carved jade rounds/glass discs) were used on both sides of the necklace but are inserted in an altered arrangement. The blue color of the amazonite drops complements the deep gold and yellow hues of the necklace. Even the pendant falls slightly off center, yet there is a sense of balance overall.

The large, flat, round agate pendant bead has a unique graphic quality and serves as a perfect focal point. But the unexpected ingredient is the buttery knotted leather bead! I embellished it with Bali silver spacers and tube beads. It's like slipping a gorgeous new ring on your necklace. You could employ this same technique using glass and vintage beads or gemstones. I can't emphasize enough how essential it is to think outside the box and try something new. Alter conventional bead combinations; think about coupling pearls with lapis, turquoise with crystal, African trade beads with vintage components. Be outrageous! It does not always "gel" as expected, but you won't know until you try.

This art journal page exudes a "springtime" flavor. The journal's intricate bird nest is reinvented as the knotted leather bead ring, each bead standing at attention like three baby birds chirping for their food. The cluster of amazonite briolettes denotes spring's perpetual showers. Even though white appears to dominate the page, it is gloriously contrasted with shades of yellows, greens and blues . . . colors which are easily associated with the season of renewal. Considering this color palette, beads such as the pale yellow jade rondelles, deep golden carved jade rounds and the milky blue amazonite drops were excellent choices for this necklace, all of which emanate the season of rebirth and look wonderful next to each other.

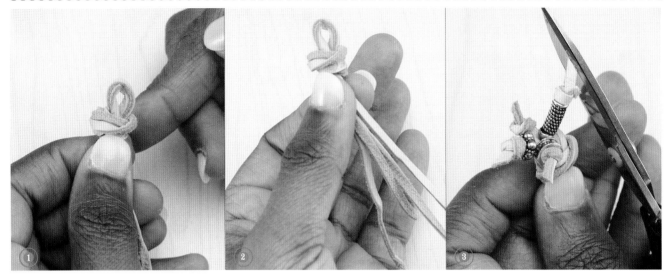

MATERIALS

(Items in **bold** are needed for the stepped-out technique)

Stringing wire

Golden carved jade rounds

Yellow jade rondelles

Powdered glass discs

Copper pearls

Amazonite drops

Tan leather lacing, 2' (61cm) (Silver Creek Leather)

Brown seed beads

Bali bead caps

Bali spacers

Sterling silver tube beads

Sterling silver seed beads

Orange vintage bead

Round flat fire crab agate beads, 2

Headpins

Chain, 4" (10cm)

Sterling silver toggle clasp

TOOLS
Scissors

KNOTTED BEAD

Want to add an unexpected component to your piece? Create a leather bead "ring" and enhance with silver spacers and tube beads.

1. Cut a 2' (61cm) length of leather and fold it in half twice. Leaving about a ½" (13mm) loop, tie a knot at the loop end.

2. Cut the loop at the other end, leaving four individual strands.

3. Thread one bead onto each strand and tie a knot at the end of each bead to secure it. Snip off the excess leather, leaving about ½" (13mm) tail. The loop end is then threaded onto the necklace.

SUCCESSFUL ASYMMETRICAL DESIGN:

- *Achieve "informal" balance by providing equally remarkable yet distinct elements within a piece.*

- *Pay attention to where your eye falls when viewing the piece. Does it move evenly around the necklace or remain focused on one area, if the latter is the case, it is probably not balanced.*

- *Distribute similar color hues or, conversely, make a statement by injecting bold color contrast (pair colors which are opposite each other on the color wheel).*

- *Eliminate the center point.*

- *Keep the center point; however, carry over and use common elements in a varied context on either side of it.*

- *Play with different kinds of beads that share similar shape.*

- *Have fun with the juxtaposition of textures.*

- *Play with pattern. I like to position beads (that have the same shape but are otherwise dissimilar) based on their size in an ascending sequence, going from small to large. I particularly enjoy employing this effect with beads that have a rondelle or disc shape. In other words, apply the same pattern sequence and bead shape, but use different beads (see Home necklace page 40).*

- *Insert one extraordinary bead (at an angle . . . not centered) that takes the piece to another level, such as the green turquoise bead in the Autumn necklace (see page 30).*

    Learn more about variations on this design style by studying the bead placement of many of the pieces throughout this book. Take a risk and depart, if only momentarily, from the safe haven of symmetrical protocol.

Spring

An interpretation of the season of rebirth. The funky asymmetrical placement of images resonates in the design of the necklace.

Ancient Voices Necklace
This necklace is inspired by the journal art on page 29; it is a variation on the Dangles on Knotted Lariat technique (see page 100).

TREE

Join the Ancients
by June Roman

Somewhere, the voices come from before,
Their song clings confidentially to soaring bark,
Happy leaves dance to the notes inscribed
within their veins.
Listen, go quietly to that place above the mountain top.
What will you do in the next life?
Join the ancients for mulberry tea?
Be the wind that ripples the water?
Hush!
Surpass the stillness you seek.

I must admit, I feel immediately present when poised in front of a tree for any length of time. When doodling, I always manage to create a basic trunk with branches, roots and leaves. I do not think that I am alone in this endeavor.

Artists have long enjoyed painting the details of peeling birch. Siddhartha sat beneath the Bodhi tree, attained enlightenment and became the Buddha. Lovers kiss under their green swathe and affectionately emboss a promise within a carved heart, while others simply exploit their shade for more practical purposes.

What fascinates me the most about these towering beauties is their longevity. The older taller trees have been around for centuries. Why does a tree live longer than we do? They have been witnesses to all of our mistakes and shortcomings, for centuries—surely they've learned something. Yes, maybe the ancient wise ones recorded the truth within their leaves and the dancing gesture they produce is their native tongue.

VISUALLY MAPPING YOUR IDEAS

So how do I translate thoughts such as these into tactile elements that I can use on a journal page? Using "Join the Ancients" as my muse, if I were to visually map my stream-of-consciousness it would look something like this:

Images: trees • leaves • ancient text • prayer • mountain • God • Buddha • water

Word combinations: wisdom • secrets • prayer • eternal life • seek stillness • seek wisdom • ancient voices

Colors and textures: waxy surfaces • crackled textures • stamped wax • tree bark • twigs • rust • umber • greens • blues

Mixed-media materials: ancient writings • old text • old maps • mica • wax • rubber stamp images • watercolor • Shiva paint sticks • crackle paste

Emotions/thought process: stillness • calm • mindfulness • centered • peace

Mapping ideas can be stimulating for any type of art. Using the above "art starters" for the Ancient Voices journal page, I selected various leaf charms based on the content from the poem. The engraved jade rounds were inspired by the Chinese symbols on the page (page 29). The earthy color combination is carried over to the large leather knotted jasper donut, dark brown wooden cup beads, juicy green turquoise ovals, bone rondelles, ancient-"looking" copper charms and even the huge quirky coconut bead! When selecting materials for your jewelry piece, pull color, content and texture directly from the art journal page.

I am the forest's conscience, but remember the forest eats itself and lives forever.
—*Barbara Kingsolver*, **The Poisonwood Bible**

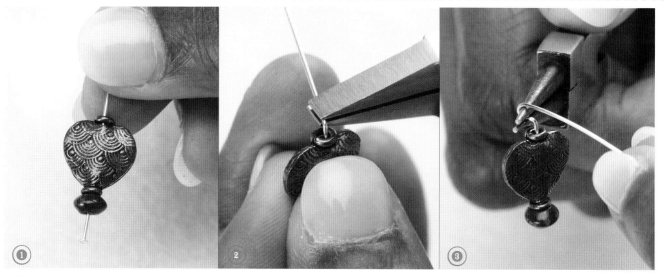

MATERIALS

(Items in **bold** are needed for the stepped-out technique)

STRAND

Stringing wire

Dark-brown wooden cup beads

Dark-brown wooden round beads

Wooden saucer beads

Sterling silver seed beads

Turquoise ovals

Carved jade bead

Coconut beads, 2 large

Jasper disc, 1 large

Coral stick bead

Mookaite stick bead

Dark brown jasper rondelles

Copper toggle clasp

Crimp tubes

Crimp covers (optional)

FOCAL DONUT BEAD

Jasper donut bead, large

Leather lacing, 2' (61cm) (Silver Creek Leather)

Various large-hole beads to string onto leather lacing

Silver leaf charms (Hill Tribe)

Copper bead

Jump ring

Headpins, 2" (5cm)

TOOLS

Flat-nose pliers

Round-nose pliers

Bent chain-nose pliers

Flush cutters

Scissors

KNOTTED LEATHER DONUT WITH CHARMS

This technique is a lovely way to enhance an ordinary gemstone donut bead, Chinese coin (see page 117) or any bead that is flat and has a hole. Even though I have used this technique as a centered focal piece in this necklace, it does not mean this always has to be the case. Think out of the box when it comes to bead placement. I have inserted accent pieces to the left or right of the center point to add interest. Just remember that the rest of the beads on the strand must be balanced and harmonize in color, size and shape.

MAKE A CHEAT SHEET

Scan a copy of your art page (or take a digital photo of it) and upload the image to your computer. Print out a color copy and take it with you when you are ready to go shopping for your beads. Use it as a reference when selecting your materials.

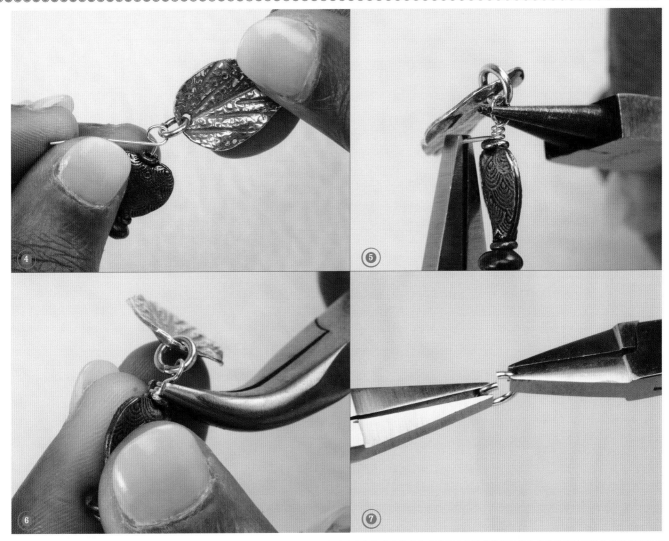

1. Thread a small bead onto a 2" (5cm) head-pin to act as a stopper and then add a larger bead.

2. Make a bend in the pin just beyond the large bead.

3. Use round-nose pliers to create a loop just after the bend.

4. Finish the loop, then thread a small charm onto the loop.

5. Grasp the loop in chain-nose pliers and wrap the tail of the wire around the base of the loop a couple of times.

6. Trim the excess wire using flush cutters, then cinch in the end of the wire to make a smooth wrap, using chain-nose pliers.

7. Open a 9mm jump ring, using two pairs of chain-nose pliers. To open the ring, use a slight twisting motion, rather than pulling the ring straight apart.

POETRY IN NATURE

If expressing spiritual ideas is difficult for you, try accessing this realm through nature. A simple walk through the woods can put one in touch with unlimited possibilities for inspiration. Stand quietly and watch birds in flight, examine a nest, look intently at a running brook, appreciate the geometry of a pine cone; notice nature's symmetry and imitate it in your work. If you do not consider yourself a poet, then borrow some of your favorites from poets both past and present and brainstorm ideas for a collage based on the content.

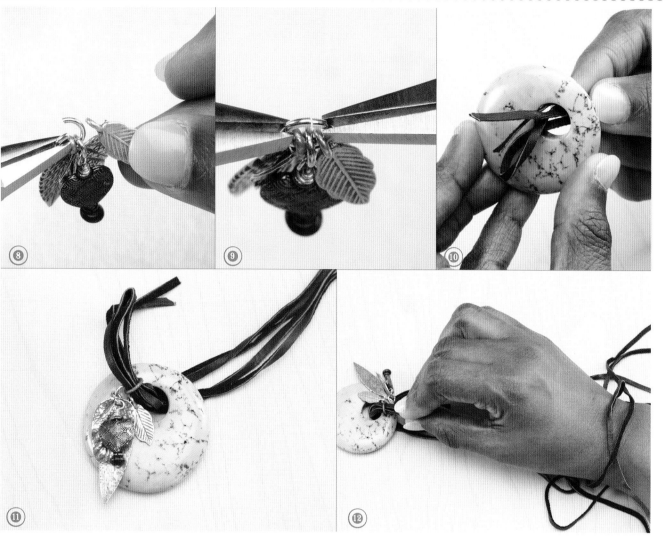

8. Thread on the wrapped dangle and two other charms.

9. Use the chain-nose pliers to close the jump ring. I shimmy the ring back and forth with the pliers to make the closure tight. Add a second jump ring to the one you just closed.

10. Trim a length of leather cord to about 2' (61cm). Fold it in half and then in half again. Thread the half that has two tails and one loop through the large donut.

11. Thread the leather bundle through the end jump ring from step 9.

12. Now, pull the end with the charms (the entire bundle) through the pair of loops that make up the rest of the length of the leather.

13. Pull the leather taut.

14. Separate the two tail ends and the two loop ends and, with the two pairs, tie one overhand knot.

15. Tie one large knot with the entire bundle. Pull the knot as close to the previous knot as possible.

16. Using scissors, snip the remaining loop so that you have a total of four individual strands.

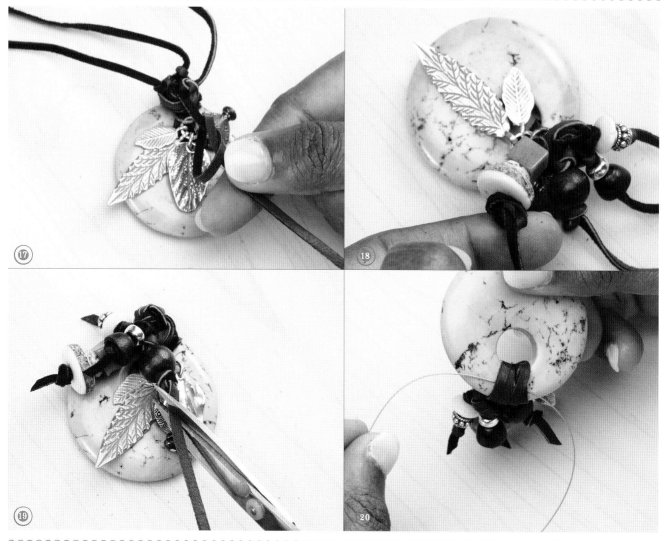

17. Tie a knot on each strand, working the knots as close to the large knot as possible.

18. Thread beads—however many/whatever size you like—onto the individual strands. This is much easier if you use large-hole beads. After threading on the beads, tie another knot on each strand to secure them. If desired, tie an additional knot on each individual strand, again working the knots as close to the existing knots as possible.

19. Snip the ends of each strand, leaving about a ⅛" (3mm) tail.

20. Determine the length you want your necklace to be by wrapping the wire directly off of the spool around your neck. I like to leave about 6" (15cm) extra wire after that to work with. Thread the wire through the four strands on the back of the donut. You can now string the rest of your necklace however you desire.

MAKE A POINT

To make threading leather through beads easier, snip the end to a sharp point using sharp scissors.

Join the Ancie

Somewhere, the voices com from
Their song clings confidentially to bark.
Happy leaves dance to the notes inscribe with their veins.
They say, Listen, you can hear us, go quietly to that place above the mountain top.
They ask, What will you do in the next life?
Join the ancients for mulberry tea
Be the wind that ripples the wat
Hush!
Surpass the stillness you seek

Ancient Voices

Playing with crackle paste, watercolor and Shiva paint sticks enabled the artist to achieve the look of ancient paper. Other "ancient" elements include waxed papers, old text, stamped images and textured papers. Tree necklace steals its "leaves," Asian symbolism and colors precisely from the journal page.

AUTUMN

There is a particular birch that stands alone on its own tiny island of concrete. Every autumn, completely indifferent to its prison, this birch boasts the most luscious golden-yellow leafage you have ever seen. On first sight, I immediately succumb to sadness, knowing winter's eerie approach will quickly abscond with its gorgeous cloak. However, I do not dwell on this fact for long. This time of year brings with it pleasant days and cool nights—a reprieve from the scorching hot and humid days of a Georgia summer. Perhaps this is another reason why this birch and I are simpatico, and therefore, why I must capture its essence in a journal page.

Using oxide yellows, reds and hints of green fluid acrylics, I forge ahead layering paint, text and texture onto small grids which remind me of my birch's cement home. I am pleased with the results as the completed page is an abstract representation of my muse. How can I move from this page to a jewelry piece? I always begin with color; however, I know it will be difficult to find beautiful opaque yellow gemstones to symbolize the foliage. Citrine is certainly gorgeous, but it is too ethereal to replicate the solidity of my birch.

Discovering this strand of yellow jasper was indeed a remarkable find. After that, it did not take long to locate the rest of the components for this piece. The lovely glass discs harmonize perfectly with their range of fall-like colors. The coral "branch" was an obvious choice, and my coveted uniquely shaped turquoise bead had been waiting for a place to fit in for a long time. An entire necklace of this oddly shaped turquoise bead might be too much of a good thing; however, used alone on a strand of commonly colored beads results in a huge statement. This bead jumps out, says "hello," and is confident enough to stand on its own due to its beautiful striations, rare multifaceted color and odd island-like shape—all attributes that mirror my birch. You should always try to find a bead that will distinguish your piece and make it extraordinary. Do you find yourself fumbling with an unusual bead and ultimately put it down thinking, "I'm never going to use this"? That's the exact bead you should purchase! You will eventually find a special place for it in your work.

I wanted to make the coral branch a focal point, so, instead of just placing it in the front of my necklace, I decided to give it a function. Transforming it into a toggle was the solution, and, after struggling with the prototype for awhile, I figured out how to do it successfully.

Even though an art journal page can provide unlimited inspiration, locating the exact components for a piece may take some time; therefore, patience is required. The results will be well worth the wait.

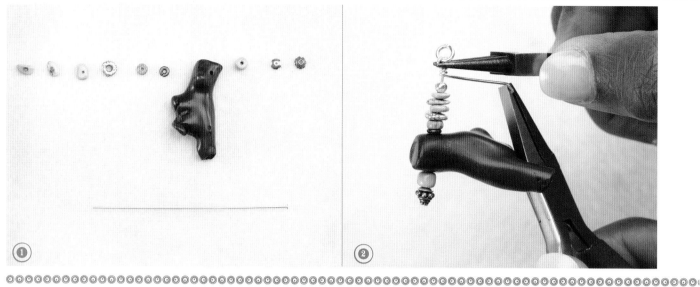

① ②

MATERIALS

(Items in **bold** are needed for the stepped-out technique)

CORAL TOGGLE

Coral branch
Bali silver spacer
Stamped silver ring
Copper ring or washer
Nacazori pueblo bead
Nacazori chips
Primavera disc
Headpin, 20-gauge, 3" (8cm)

CHARMS

Tibetan turquoise bead with silver caps
Sterling silver leaf charm
Glass disc
Silver spacer
Primavera disc
20-gauge silver wire
Headpins

LARIAT

Silver seed beads (Hill Tribe Silver beads are wonderful)
Carico Lake turquoise chips, 3
Small jump ring
Primavera disc
Crimp tube
Crimp cover

NECKLACE STRAND

Strand of yellow jasper
Stringing wire

Glass disc beads (Blue Healer Glass)
Red carved cinnabar bead
Coral stick
Small coral rounds, 3
Stamped silver ring
Coral disc
Large odd-shaped turquoise bead
Large ornate Bali bead
Turquoise bead
Silver saucer bead
Crimp beads
Crimp covers
Faded green seed beads

TOOLS

Chain-nose pliers
Round-nose pliers
Flush cutters
Crimping pliers

CORAL TOGGLE

This technique demonstrates how to create an unusual toggle that works double duty as a focal pendant. Get creative by devising a new purpose for an for an object from that which was originally intended for it.

1. Lay out your elements that are going to be threaded onto the 3" (7cm) headpin.

2. Beginning with a Bali spacer, thread on all of the elements. Use chain-nose pliers to make a bend in the wire at the end of the beads, then create a loop with round-nose pliers. Thread on an 18-gauge closed jump ring and close the loop by wrapping the excess wire around the base of the loop.

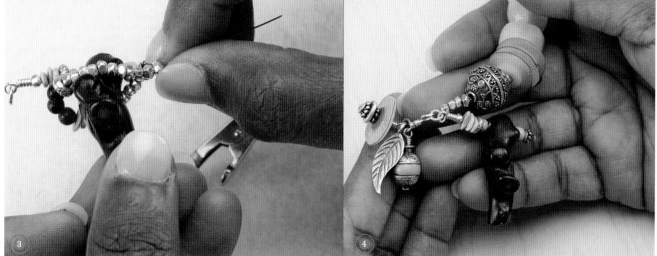

3. To create a lariat for the piece of coral, start by stringing small beads, on coated wire, guesstimating how many beads it will take to go around the widest part of the coral. When you think it's about right, test it by wrapping it around. It should be snug but not too tight.

4. If you need to add or remove beads, do so. Then add a crimp tube. After crimping the tube, add a crimp cover or slightly larger silver bead. String the rest of your necklace as desired. When you are at the end, it's time to add your coral toggle.

T IS FOR TOGGLE

Select your coral branch bead carefully. Choose a branch that is no longer than 1½" (4cm) for comfort sake, with a hole drilled at the top so that it can be turned into a "T" formation. Also, you do not want the branch to be completely smooth but for it to have bumps and ridges like a real tree branch. This gives the lariat a place to rest so that it does not slip off. Use a series of varying colored small beads, spacers, rings and washers to complete the crossbar and add interest to the toggle.

Autumn

The gridded autumn landscape is an abstract representation of my muse, the birch tree. Each year it boasts the most brilliant yellow foliage causing onlookers to gasp in amazement. My Autumn necklace serves as a yearly reminder of its beauty.

ORGANIC ELEMENTS

Picasso's words are so true. Inspiration can come from countless places; therefore it behooves us to pay attention. The inspiration for the Organic Elements necklace did not begin with an art journal page. In fact, quite the opposite occurred.

One day, while visiting a favorite local bead store, I happened to see a grouping of small cowrie shells in a dish. I loved their milky beige color and organic shape, even the inner portion of the shell presented interesting curves and a deeper color variation. I checked to see if stringing material could be inserted but I did not locate any hole and I wasn't sure how I would use these shells in jewelry design, still, I had to have them.

After some contemplation I decided I liked the idea of using the shell in a collage setting; however, its unusual shape and size would not allow it to be completely encased within a bezel. But why should that matter? Creating a three-dimensional collage would add tactile and architectural interest to this piece.

Next, I gathered the rest of my elements. When selecting your items for collage consider how they will appear if magnified. Resin magnifies the details of any piece it covers; consequently, this phenomena could have very interesting possibilities. The inside portion of a small daisy (the pistil) contains extremely tiny details; therefore, it appears quite mysterious under resin. Hence, I plucked all of the petals off my little daisy!

I was very pleased with the look of the completed bezel and, once it was finished curing, I took it with me to select the rest of the beads for the necklace. A beige strand of jasper, although beautiful, was quickly set aside as too boring. I needed a strand that would add a subtle contrast but still have a natural appearance to support the organic direction I was taking. The umber-colored painted jasper rondelles were my beads of choice. In addition, the striped vintage glass bead was the surprise pick for this piece. Many would have thought it too polished for such an earthy design. However, I believe this bead makes a strong statement which is why I incorporated the Infinity Twist technique (see page 78) to draw even more attention to it. Who says you should only have one focal setting in a necklace? As you can see, having more than one works as long as all of the elements are balanced and the colors are within the same palette.

After naming the piece, Organic Elements, I was excited about executing a journal page of the same name. I rummaged through my stash of decorative papers to locate images that echoed the natural nuances of my jewelry piece. The inspiration for this entire piece originated from a tiny shell, a "passing shape" which Picasso spoke of so eloquently. In this case, the necklace came before the art journal page and the results are stunning!

The artist is a receptacle for emotions that come from all over the place: from the sky, from the earth, from a scrap of paper, from a passing shape, from a spider's web.
—Picasso

MATERIALS

(Items in **bold** are needed for the stepped-out technique)

NECKLACE

Stringing wire

Painted jasper rondelles

Large resin carnelian bead
Vintage glass bead
Amazonite rounds
Faceted sterling silver beads
White glass rounds
Bone discs
Sterling silver "S" clasp

PENDANT

Bezel (Nunn Designs)

Crackle Paste (Golden)

Found text

Distress Ink (Tim Holtz)

Dried daisy

Gel medium

Watercolor (light and dark colors)

Small shell

ICE Resin (Objects and Elements), including mixing cups and craft stick

TOOLS

Tweezers

Paintbrush

LOCATING BEZELS

Locating nice bezels can be a challenge, particularly if you are unable to make your own. I have discovered several online sites that offer them in different styles, shapes, metals and sizes (see Resources, page 124).

CHARMS

Amazonite
Bali spacers
Small silver seed beads
Jump ring
Headpins

LARIATS (Infinity twist technique page 78)

Various size sterling silver beads
Various size silver seed beads
Brown seed beads
Amazonite rondelles
Silver discs
Silver saucer bead

THREE-DIMENSIONAL COLLAGE

The next time you want to create a collage within a bezel and your items don't exactly fit, think about crafting a three-dimensional collage. The right item can add texture, color and architectural interest to any piece.

1. Scoop out some Crackle Paste to fill your bezel. Smooth it out using a palette knife or your finger.

2. Distress some found text with Distress Ink. I like to just use my fingers to push it onto the pad.

3. Tear the edges of the text however you like and then lightly press it into the paste in the bezel. Use tweezers to reposition it if necessary.

4. I wanted to use just the center of a dried daisy, so I pulled the petals off with tweezers. You can use any dried flowers you like.

   Position the flower over part of the text paper, adhering it with just a small dot of gel medium.

6. Set the bezel aside to allow the paste to dry. Apply a coat of watercolor paint to the dried bezel. Here, I used a lighter color to begin with, then added a darker color in places to seep into the cracks for further depth.

7. Glue on a shell that is higher than the depth of the bezel, using gel medium.

8. Mix up a small batch of resin (see page 16) and pour it over your dried collage, being mindful not to get excess resin on the shell where it extends beyond the resin.

Organic Elements

The merging of abstract shapes, rich earthy hues and textured surfaces echoes the subtle nuances of the resin-covered centerpiece. Borrowing actual elements from nature, as I did within the bezel, imparts an unrefined elegance, thus adding images of plants, sealife and insects to the journal page continues the theme.

A SENSE OF PLACE

How difficult is it to find a sense of place in a world whose mission is to keep us continually connected? Even though we treasure the conveniences of cell phones, Wi-Fi and Bluetooth, do we not sometimes grow weary of the continual buzz that signals yet another text message, E-mail or Facebook communication?

In this chapter we will be exploring themes that focus on our sense of place. What connects you to this earth? Where do you feel most at home? Being rooted within our environment gives us the stability and security required to thrive. Without it we may as well float like a feather above the atmosphere, having no particular place to roost; thereby, unable to fulfill our true purpose.

When my daughter was four years old, she participated in an interview process to be accepted into an established Montessori school. During the process, she was asked to draw a picture of herself. After the interview was over, I was called in to discuss her results. The interviewer pulled out the picture she had drawn. It was a lovely full-page rendition of herself standing in grass. "My," the interviewer remarked, "She is completely grounded!" To say the least, I was very proud and happy that my little one felt a strong sense of place at such a tender age. It parallels my own experience detailed in "Sky" (see page 46).

At times it is necessary to step away from the technology that keeps our minds constantly stimulated and focused on everything except the present moment. Where do you go to reflect? A mind that stays on fast-forward loses its ability to think creatively. How can we extract ideas from our environment if we are not deeply connected to it? Find your sense of place, wherever it may be, and get in touch with who you really are.

A knowledge of place is grounded in those aspects of the environment which we appreciate through the senses, color, texture, slope, quality of light, the feel of wind, the sounds and scents carried by that wind.

—Kent Rydan

HOME

Several years ago I participated in an online group entitled Finding Water. Julia Cameron's book of the same title outlines a twelve-week program intended to help artists renew and evolve artistically. We worked through a series of exercises geared to tap into our artistic abilities and shared our experiences by presenting our "homework" as well as commenting on each other's blog. I found this to be a very convenient way to participate in a meaningful workshop, and, by doing so, gained much insight on the creative process within the human psyche.

One of the exercises in Finding Water asked us to think of ourselves as a character in a book or movie. Often we become fascinated by the main character of a novel and Julia believes we should be as equally fascinated with ourselves. Writing a mini biography about ourselves in third person is an excellent way to begin this process. The following writing activity served as the trigger for the Journey Back art page.

"She thinks it odd to live so close to a mountain where deer run free because instead of residing in a rustic habitat, she calls a modern condo with 9-foot ceilings and hardwood floors her home. The juxtaposition of her residence and surroundings makes her smile.

"She loves the colors of her walls because they remind her of the turquoise oceans of St. Thomas. The deep red comfy sofa makes a bold statement against the sea of blue. It tickles her that the first thing people say when they walk into her home is, 'Oh! I just love the color of your living room!'

"There is an ensemble of meaningful objects that are scattered about her home: funky patchwork pillows her sister handcrafted, white dishes she received one Christmas, blue and white porcelain collectibles and her beloved ebony Indonesian hutch. 'Eclectic cottage' would probably define her style to a T.

"She's at an age she would desperately like to forget. Every now and then she notices the ever-so-slight wrinkles forming on her face. Peering into a mirror, she takes the palms of her hands, places them on each side of her face and softly moves them in an upward direction to receive the free face-lift. She reluctantly releases the upward pull and accepts the reality that passing time has on the human shell.

"She lives with a sense of optimism that blankets some self-doubt and a few insecurities. These ailments act as a low-grade fever; consequently, they do not appear to be life threatening.

"The best thing however is that for the first time in her life she knows exactly what she wants: a place to be free; time to create and a Spanish-style cottage in the hills of any city beginning with the name Santa. She sees herself walking barefoot across the cool ruddy terra-cotta tile, her white linen gown gently wraps around her legs as a breeze from an open window enters the house. She hears the soothing stream of water as it trickles from a copper fountain. She's not certain what time of year it is, most likely autumn, and the night sky is calling her, beckoning her to come outside and greet the sweet air and view the overwhelmingly beautiful evening performance. God is waiting there for her. He asks, 'Do you like the grassy green kitchen cabinets and Mexican tile countertops?' She howls with laughter nodding in the affirmative. All she has to do is believe."

Writing about myself in the third person gave me a lot of freedom to record my own story, one that certainly has achievable possibilities. I enjoy picturing my future cottage as well as imagining my life in it, and decided to represent several of its attributes in my necklace. The green ceramic focal bead symbolizes the Mexican tile countertops, the large carved wooden bead embodies my Indonesian hutch and the old African skunk bead is the same color as the terra-cotta floors. The reclaimed copper beads from a former necklace correspond to the copper waterfall. Notice the asymmetrical design of the necklace. It works because similar colors, shapes and beads were used on each side; thereby, keeping the weight of the design balanced and aesthetically pleasing to the eye (see more about asymmetrical design on page 21).

The ache for home lives in all of us, the safe place where we can go as we are and not be questioned.
—Maya Angelou

41

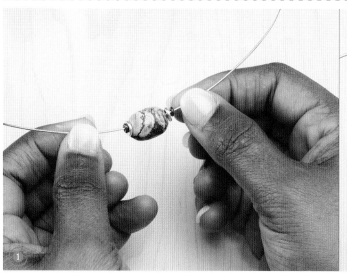
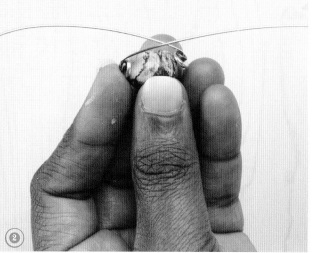

MATERIALS

(Items in **bold** are needed for the stepped-out technique)

STRAND

Stringing wire

Jasper rounds

Coconut beads, 2 large

Various-sized bone rondelles, 6

Carnelian rondelle

Small turquoise bead

Peruvian heishi bead

White howlite disc

Turquoise disc

Large antique coral rondelle

Brown seed beads

Copper bead caps, 2

African skunk bead

Nacozari turquoise pueblo bead

Sterling silver spacer beads (with holes large enough to cover a crimp tube), 2

Turquoise chips

Copper beads, 2

Leather lace

Jump rings

Headpin

Crimp tubes

Copper toggle clasp

WIRE-WRAPPED BEAD FOR CLASP

20-gauge wire, 7" (18cm)

Jasper barrel bead

Bali silver spacer

Bone rondelles, 2 small

Small primavera rondelle

Sterling silver charms, 2

Small sterling silver rings, 2

LARIATS

Stamped silver seed beads

Stamped silver ring

Small turquoise round

Small copper bead cap

CLUSTER BEADS

Large flat round turquoise bead

Small bone rondelle

Carnelian oval bead

Turquoise chips

Silver seed beads

Length of chain, 4" (10cm)

Small turquoise bead

Small copper bead cap

Headpins

FOCAL BEAD

Large rectangle ceramic bead

Small turquoise beads, 2

Silver spacer beads, 2

Headpin, 3" (8cm)

Jump ring

TOOLS

Round-nose pliers

Chain-nose pliers

Flush cutters

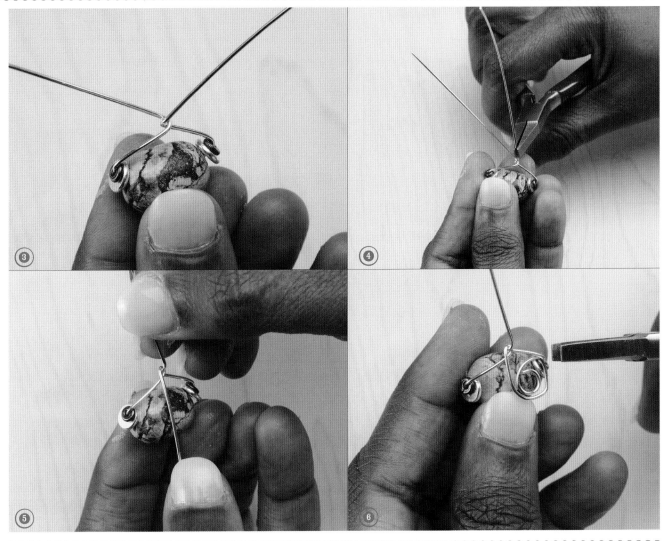

WIRE-WRAPPED BEAD

Adding a distinctive charm to a clasp makes the back of a necklace as interesting as the front.

1. Cut a 7" (18cm) length of 20-gauge wire and thread it through a large bead. Also thread some small rings onto both sides of the bead.

2. Fold both halves of the wire all the way over to their other sides.

3. Twist the two wires together.

4. Bend one wire up straight, using chain-nose pliers.

5. Bend the other wire perpendicular with the previous wire.

6. Create a spiral from the wire you just bent down, using round-nose pliers to begin the spiral, then switching to chain-nose pliers to continue for the length of the wire. You may wish to trim off some of the wire first if it's longer than 2" (5cm).

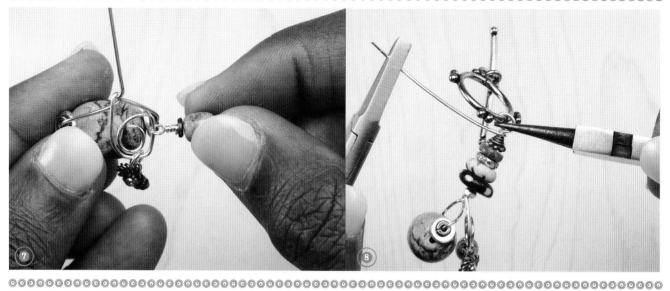

7. Thread a couple of charms or dangles onto the spiral.

8. Thread a few beads on the remaining wire and create a wrapped loop at the top after threading on your clasp.

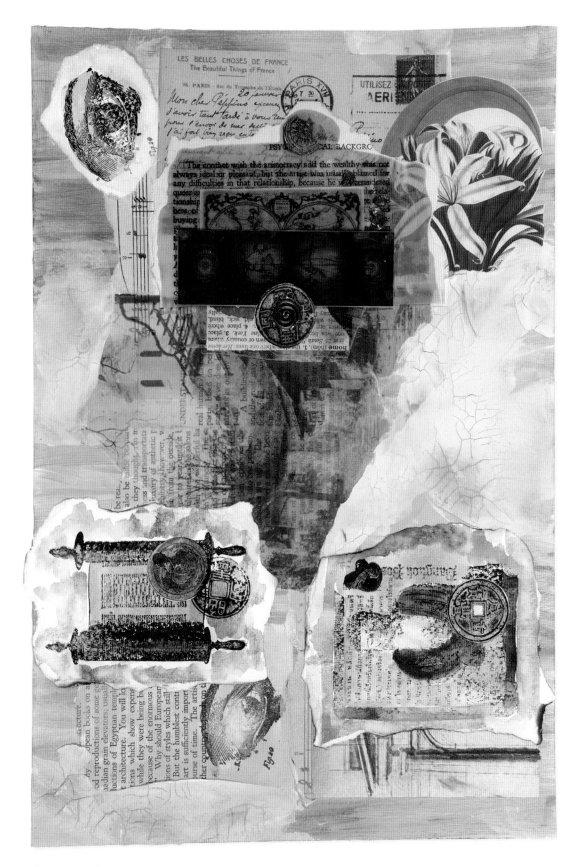

Journey Back

This page encompasses many of the aspects of home that I deem essential: creating an environment filled with peace, music, rich color, ancient books and a superfluity of art/writing tools.

SKY

Picasso said, "All children are artists. The problem is how to remain an artist once he grows up." As a child, I can remember lying face up in my bed with a slight smile on my face, appreciating the initial indications of a bright summer morning. The steady stream of fresh air filled my tiny nostrils, sunshine illuminated every surface, and I could hear the faint sounds of giddy laughter and chatter from children playing down by the creek. I slowly emerged from my sweet slumber, while simultaneously calculating the possibilities of the day, all before my feet even touched the hardwood floors. I was excited about what the day had in store for me, never doubting it would be brilliant.

I was not intimidated by the box of sixty-four Crayola colors, nor did I worry about what I would sculpt with my Play-Doh, and good Lord, as soon as I could get outside to greet the day there was no need for Parker Brothers to govern my adventures. I made up my own games and, more importantly, my own rules. There were instances when this unbridled creativity led to my downfall, such as the famous (or should I say infamous) "Toilet Paper Parade." I don't know why I thought it would be a good idea to tie this utilitarian material on sticks, and encourage a host of friends to do likewise. The inspiration for the parade quickly ensued and we all jumped on our bikes, held our handmade flags proudly in the air and took our procession to the streets, to the horror and dismay of my poor mother. Needless to say, we never made those flags again, but it was a delicious idea at the time. I was not in survival mode back then; life was easy . . . life was fun.

The creative spirit resides deep within and even as a young child I would lay still in the grass with my head resting upon cradled arms, look up at the bluest sky, and for a fleeting moment realize there was something much bigger than myself at work in the universe. As adults we tend to forget how important it is to just be still, to be quiet and know without any uncertainty that anything is possible. This simple act gives birth to the seeds of greatness.

Recalling childhood memories is the basis of inspiration for the Sky journal page and ultimately the necklace. Think about those past moments that made you the happiest. What season of the year was it? What colors come to mind? How did this occasion touch your heart? Use the answers to these questions to facilitate possible ideas for a journal page and ultimately a unique piece of jewelry.

Peering longingly into the vastness of the bluest sky harkens back to one of the most profound experiences of my childhood. How could I not seize the opportunity to create something special from it? A tribute of this memory fits snugly into the confines of a bezel which hangs from strands of large turquoise discs which happen to be as blue as the sky! Who would think of pairing crystal with turquoise? Out-of-the-ordinary bead combinations result in unique design possibilities. Think about ways to accomplish this in your own work.

Even though the restrictiveness of our daily schedules tend to crowd out our precious playtime, it is important to take the time to nourish our spirit, continually engage in creative pursuits, and courageously conceive the impossible!

. . . And the bluest ink
Isn't really sky
And at times I think
I would gladly die
For a day of sky
—Stephen Sondheim, "I Remember"

MATERIALS

(Items in **bold** are needed for the stepped-out technique)

NECKLACE

Stringing wire

Large turquoise discs

Turquoise seed beads

Amazonite rondelles

Turquoise rounds

Nacozari turquoise pueblo cut beads

Silver seed beads

Small silver rondelles

Silver spacers, 4

Bali silver bead caps, 3

Carved jade bead

Glass flower bead

Bali beads, 2

Small flower charm

Sterling silver toggle clasp

Crimps

Crimp covers

PENDANT

Large silver bezel (Nunn Designs)

Bird diagrams from old dictionary

Text from old dictionary

Crackle Paste (Golden)

Watercolor paint

Small dried flower

Gel medium

ICE Resin (Objects and Elements), including mixing cups and stir stick

CHAIN DANGLES

Swarovski crystal cube

Vintage chandelier crystal

Bali bead

Karico Lake turquoise chips

Sterling silver chain, 2" (5cm)

20-gauge wire, 4½" (11cm)

Headpins

TOOLS

Diagonal flush cutters

Flat-nose pliers

Round-nose pliers

Paintbrush

Tweezers

JUMPSTARTING CREATIVITY

What happens when our creative juices suddenly and unexpectedly run dry? As a jewelry designer, I ponder this dilemma, albeit only momentarily. I have several quick fixes under my belt. Here are some suggestions to help you through those unproductive periods that haunt us all.

- *Commit to taking time out of your day, preferably very early in the morning before anyone else is awake, to be quiet and at peace, even meditate if the spirit moves you to do so.*

- *The space in which you work needs to be comfortable as well as inspirational. Hang pictures of images that kindle the imagination, paint the walls your favorite color, and place your special pieces in prominent locations throughout the space.*

- *Go for nature walks, they are refreshing and you will be surprised by the things that inspire you along the way.*

- *Engage in artistic pursuits other than your chosen medium. Even though I am passionate about jewelry design and mixed media, I also write, paint and sew.*

- *Go with the flow. Creativity is an elusive process that ignites unexpectedly and, if you allow it, will flow continually. When an extraordinary idea explodes, yield immediately, let it overtake you, and remove any egotistical leanings. It is not about you, it is about the process. Creating really is a form of surrender. For me, it often takes place in the wee hours of the morn, while I am putting a bead on, taking a bead off, until I am no longer thinking, just doing, and that's when something genuine becomes form. Once the trance is broken, I may as well walk away until the next providential urge to create takes over. I live for those moments.*

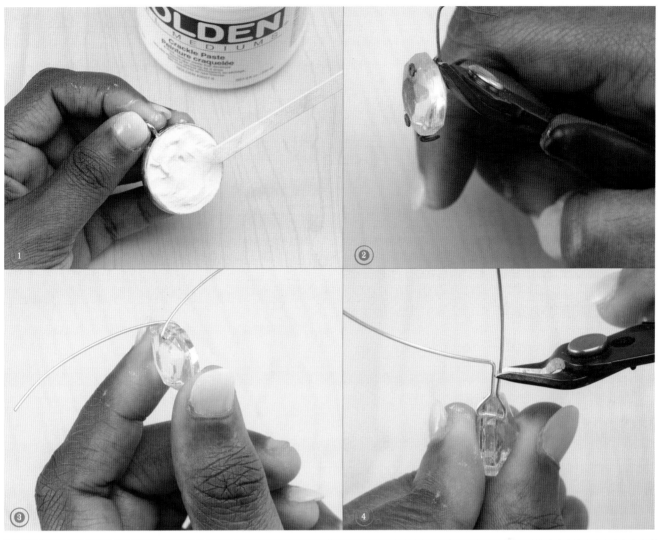

COLLAGE ON CRACKLE PASTE

Filling bezels with crackle paste offers jewelry artists a unique way to present collage elements. Cover the finished product with resin to protect the contents.

1. Fill your bezel with Golden Crackle Paste and create some peaks and texture on the surface with a stir stick or your finger.

2. Set the bezel aside to dry. If you wish to use crystals from an old chandelier or piece of jewelry, first remove the old wire.

3. Wash the crystal with mild soap and water. Insert a length of 20-gauge wire through the crystal and ease both ends of the wire together so that they cross at the top of the crystal.

4. Bend one wire up, using pliers, and wrap the other wire around it once. Snip the excess wire.

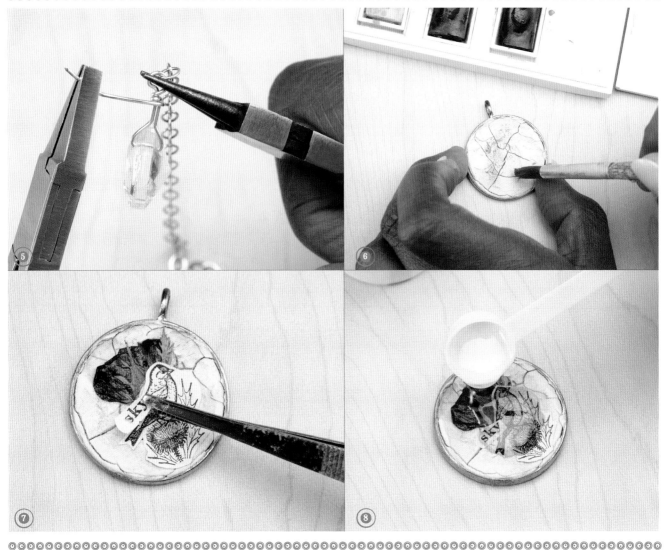

5. Create a loop above the wrap, using round-nose pliers. Thread the loop onto a jump ring or existing chain and wrap the excess wire around the base of the loop. Snip the excess wire.

6. Paint the dried crackle paste in the bezel using either watercolor like I am, or watered-down acrylic. Use as few or as many colors as you like.

7. After the paint has dried, begin your collage by clipping out some found text and/or images that you like. Here I am also including a dried flower that I first sealed with gel medium. Add your elements to the painted bezel using gel medium.

8. Mix up a small batch of resin (see page 16) and pour it over your dried collage.

VISUAL MAP

If I were to visually graph the symbols for this piece, it would look something like this:

Images: *sky • clouds • bird • nest*

Word combinations: *fearless • free • I Remember Sky • vastness of sky*

Colors and textures: *sky blue • white • weaved textures • twigs • branches*

Mixed-media materials: *fluid acrylic paints • weaved art papers • crumbled tissue paper • crackle paste • Shiva paint sticks • bird/nest images*

Emotions/thought process: *fearless • peace • unbridled joy • childhood memories • profound spiritual moment*

Beading materials/ideas: *turquoise (the color of sky) • turquoise chips • crystals (on a clear day you can see forever) • wire bird nest • bird charms • deep blue Nacozari beads • collage bird pendant with crackle paste (capture memories) • dictionary text/diagrams*

I Remember Sky

A whimsical rendition of my childhood "sky" captured in collage format. The components of the necklace are lovingly expressed through color, text and pictures.

SECRET

I love designing with rare semiprecious gemstones even though my pocketbook doesn't always allow me that pleasure. Among my favorites are blue garnets, Mohave turquoise, Mexican fire opal and the deep purple opaque sugalite stone, which happens to be featured in the Secret choker. Rarely can you find a stone that naturally sports a stunning opaque color without it having been dyed. The quality of a stone can either make or break a design; therefore, it is amazing when you can splurge every once in a while on something rare and wonderful.

If I only have a small number of a rare or expensive bead, I try to accentuate its presence by featuring it as a focal point, subsequently complementing the rest of the necklace with another type of bead that is equally beautiful but of lesser cost value. In this case, I grouped the sugalite rondelles with the deep purple pearls in a cluster arrangement which falls nicely from the center of the neck. This brings instant attention to the distinct sugalite beads.

Inserting tiny seed beads in-between each pearl gives it a "knotted pearl" look without having to do the knotting! This technique also allows the strands of a necklace to fall loosely avoiding that "stiff" look that might have come from the beads strung one next to each other. I also incorporated ornate Bali beads and sterling silver seed beads within the design, which adds even more sophistication to this piece. All of the sterling silver findings in this piece have been darkened with liver of sulfur solution (see page 60).

Purple is such an opulent color and many shades of it were infused in the art journal page entitled "Reclining Woman." This woman is obviously very comfortable in her own skin and is anchored to a sense of place both physically as well as on an emotional level. She possesses a wild spirit and is willing to take creative risks because she is passionate about her art. What could she be thinking? Since her back is turned, one is uncertain of her expression. Is she jotting surreptitious thoughts in a diary? Is she pondering a lost lover? Every woman is naturally mysterious. However, that being said, could it be possible at this precise moment she is void of thought and is simply at peace with herself? Wouldn't that be sublime?

Within every woman there is a wild and natural creature, a powerful force, filled with good instincts, passionate creativity, and ageless knowing. Her name is Wild Woman, but she is an endangered species . . .

—Dr. Clarissa Pinkola Estés Ph.D.

MATERIALS

(Items in **bold** are needed for the stepped-out technique)

STRAND AND BEADED LARIAT

Stringing wire
Deep purple pearls
Deep purple glass seed beads
Bali bead caps, 2
Ornate Bali bead
Sterling silver seed beads
Sterling silver faceted seed beads
Sterling silver rondelles, 3
Crimp tubes
Crimp covers

PENDANT CLOSURE

Ornate Bali beads, 2
Silver seed beads
3" (8cm) headpin
Small jump ring

CLUSTER BEADS

Sugalite beads

Deep purple pearls

Small link chain (Length is determined by how long you would like the cluster to be for your particular design. It is easier to manipulate a longer length of chain than is needed for your design, followed by trimming off additional length once it is threaded onto the bead wire.)

Headpins

Seed beads

TOOLS

Round-nose pliers

Chain-nose pliers

Diagonal flush cutters

CHAIN DANGLES

Creating a cluster arrangement of beads offers many design possibilities. Think about using this technique at the back of a necklace (hanging next to a clasp and falling beautifully down the neck) as well as in an earring design. Vary the length of the cluster by providing a longer or shorter length of chain. Use additional chains if you want to increase the volume of the cluster.

1. To create dangles using very tiny chain, start with a headpin and thread a couple of beads. Create a wire-wrapped loop at the top of the stack, threading it onto the end link of a tiny chain before closing it up.

2. Repeat creating headpin dangles, and continue up the chain, attaching them with a wire wrap at every other link. Continue for about six dangles.

3. Trim the chain, leaving about four links above the last dangle. Repeat to make another chain with five or six dangles. It is easier to thread the chain onto the stringing wire of your necklace before you actually trim the remaining portion of the chain. Once the chain is on the stringing wire, trim the excess chain.

CHOKER COMFORT

When designing a choker, be certain to measure the neck accurately and include within that measurement the length of the toggle or clasp. Don't forget to take into account your crimp beads. A choker should fit snugly yet not feel uncomfortable; therefore, include additional length for ease. This can be easily be accomplished by using a string to measure around the neck and indicate the clasp placement by marking the string with a Sharpie.

Reclining Woman

Is she merely resting or contemplating regrets of the past? The mysterious content of this art journal page was the impetus for the design of the Secret choker. The pearls and rare sugalite beads solicit their luxurious color from the journal page.

Broken Butterfly
This piece, left, is a variation on the liver of sulfur and PMC technique (see page 58).

WABI-SABI

I am not even going to pretend that I am capable of offering a satisfactory explanation for the term wabi-sabi. The Japanese aesthetic of finding beauty in imperfection is far too simplistic a way of explaining this somewhat ephemeral and complex concept. I say ephemeral because just when I think I totally understand it, its meaning escapes me entirely. I believe it is because wabi-sabi has more to do with the essence of the soul—an experience—rather than something tangible. The mission of wabi-sabi enthusiasts is to discover the extraordinary in the ordinary.

Finding poetry in the wrinkles on an elderly woman's face, adoring the verdigris patina on an old terra-cotta planter, appreciating the beauty of peeling paint, easily disregarding the urge to replace the rusty iron gate that leads to an untamed garden; this is the language of wabi-sabi. And yet these illustrations fall short of encapsulating its true meaning.

A wabi-sabi discovery may evoke feelings of profound inner awareness and concurrently cause one to give way to melancholy. The opposing dichotomy of wabi-sabi is precisely its mystery; consequently, it is an inward journey and the mode of transportation is not visible to the human eye.

Initially, I was drawn to this expression for a juvenile reason: I loved its rhyming cadence. After seriously studying this concept, however, I realized its characteristics resonated with my art and jewelry. Unpolished stone, vintage findings, blackened silver, ancient ethnic beads and artifacts, these are all of the objects I collect and covet. I find the attribute of asymmetry undeniably fascinating. Discerning that beauty and imperfection can live harmoniously is truly a wonderful thing.

The concept for the Wabi-Sabi necklace came directly from a photo of an old gate incorporated within the journal art you see on page 61. I wanted to create a necklace that looked ancient. What if while digging in the garden, I unearthed pieces of an old tablet? Undoubtedly, this artifact would have areas that were broken or crumbling apart. In order to replicate this scenario, I formed the tablets by rolling precious metal clay (PMC) on selected sections of two different rubber stamps to create the desired impression. Shiny silver tablets would not suffice however, so I added a patina with liver of sulfur (LOS) to give the PMC tablets an aged finish and the allure of wabi-sabi.

The calcite beads were a perfect choice for the strand because each bead had been hand-faceted in India, giving them an organic and primal quality, as opposed to the perfection of a machine-faceted stone. Each calcite bead was linked by hand-wired loop connectors instead of using stringing wire in order to maintain the archaic integrity of the piece.

Wabi-sabi is a beauty of things imperfect, impermanent, and incomplete. It is the beauty of things modest and humble. It is the beauty of things unconventional.

—Leonard Koren from his book
Wabi-Sabi: for Artists, Designers, Poets & Philosophers

① ②

MATERIALS

(Items in **bold** are needed for the stepped-out technique)

TABLETS

Precious Metal Clay (PMC standard or PMC+)

Liver of Sulfur (LOS)

Selected rubber stamps

PMC tool kit (see page 11)

Garnets/Pearls/Bali silver spacers for hanging charms

Headpins

STRAND

Calcite nuggets (hand-faceted)

Sterling silver wire that has been darkened with LOS and cut into 4" (10cm) pieces (the total amount depends on the length of the necklace and is equal to the number of nuggets you are using. The gauge of your wire is determined by the size of the holes in your beads. In this case, I used 20-gauge sterling silver wire.)

Closed jump rings that have been darkened with LOS (2 for each nugget you are using)

Toggle clasp (darkened with LOS)

BEAD CHARMS (ATTACHED TO JUMP RINGS BETWEEN EACH BEAD CONNECTOR)

Faceted garnet rounds

Silver seed beads

Small white pearls

Copper bead caps for pearls

Headpins that have been darkened with LOS

TOOLS

PMC Tool Kit (see page 11)

Round-nose pliers

LIVER OF SULFUR (LOS) AND PRECIOUS METAL CLAY (PMC)

Designing necklaces with gemstones and beads can be very satisfying; however, there are times when you may have an idea for a particular adornment that cannot be found in a store—something that is totally unique. The best way to achieve this is by designing your own embellishments with PMC. I will demonstrate a very easy way to complete freeform stamped tablets out of PMC and how to use LOS to simulate an aged surface.

1. Put just a bit of oil on your finger and then rub it over the portion of the stamp that you wish to use.

2. Work a bit of PMC Standard into a ball and then roll to a thin layer over the oiled portion, using a roller. Roll it out in both directions.

CHOOSE WISELY

Select each bead and strand meticulously. In time you will amass a distinct private collection. I select my beads the same way I choose fruit—very carefully. Jewelry that is crafted with your own hands and is inspired from art that evolves from the soul is evidence that you are on the perfect path, the one that leads through a tarnished iron gate and transports you home.

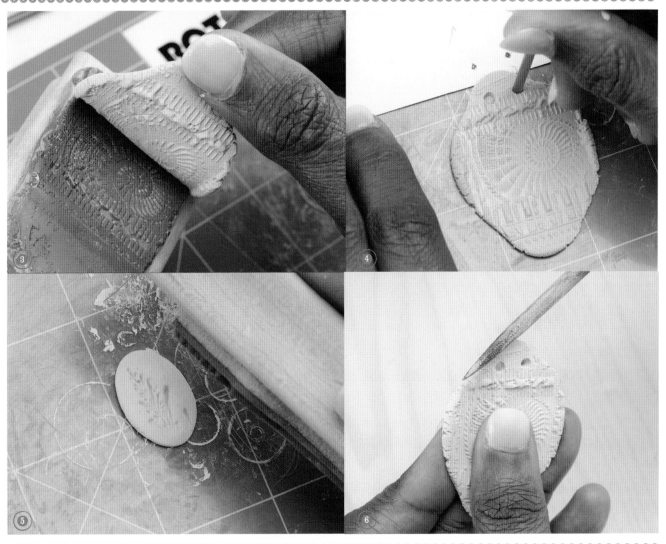

3. Gently peel it off the stamp. Repeat with a slightly smaller piece and a different stamp.

STAMP SELECTION

Choosing the correct stamp for this project is crucial. Deeply etched rubber stamps work best; however, less embossed stamps will work as well; just remember to rub a small amount of olive oil on the stamp. I only used a specific section of the stamp for my design . . . not the entire stamp; therefore locating a particular image/texture on a larger rubber stamp would be appropriate.

4. Lay each clay piece flat on your work surface and decide where you want to punch two holes at the top, using a stir straw or something similar. If you use a template, then you can make the holes the same distance apart on both tablet pieces. Punch a hole at the bottom as well, if you wish to hang a charm from it, as I did. Lay the piece on a tile or nonstick surface to dry for 24 hours.

HOLES AFTER FIRING

If you wish to create a hole in a piece made from PMC after it has been fired, you can always do so by using a drill.

5. To create some charms from PMC, roll a very small bit into a ball, then roll it out onto your work surface. Press a small stamp, such as this leaf, into the clay.

6. Punch a hole into each charm and lay them out to dry as well. When the clay is dry, and before firing it, file off any big burs with a metal file. This piece is supposed to look old and distressed, so don't worry about making it perfect!

7. After they have dried and been fired, scrub them with dish soap and a wire brush.

8. I like to patina all of my findings and elements at once. Here, I am using liver of sulfur and will blacken my PMC pieces as well as some silver seed beads, jump rings and some sterling wire. Dip a piece in for a few seconds, pull it out and look at it, then dip it more if you want it darker. I want this one to be dark.

9. I usually throw the small findings in all at one time.

EXTENDED SHELF LIFE

Use liver of sulfur that comes in the solid form rather than its liquid counterpart. The latter has a shelf life and, in my opinion, smells stronger. Always store your liver of sulfur (in any form) in a dry, dark place, as light may weaken it. Break off a small piece and place it in a cup of hot tap water. Now you are ready to dip your silver pieces and watch the magic happen!

10. With a piece of blackened wire, create a fairly big loop, using round-nose pliers, to accommodate the two tablet pieces and one charm. Thread on the pieces, then wrap the tail of the wire around the base of the loop. Repeat for the other set of holes.

11. On one wire, thread a large bead, then create a loop at the other end of the bead and thread on a closed blackened jump ring. Wrap the tail of the wire around the base of the loop.

12. Trim the excess wire and repeat for the other wire coming from the PMC pieces. Create three tiny dangles using 24-gauge headpins and a variety of beads/bead caps. Wrap these onto one jump ring.
    Repeat for the other jump ring and continue building the necklace, alternating between large wrapped beads and jump rings with tiny dangles, until you have the length you want. Also create a dangle for the bottom of the tablet.

Iron gate photo by Yeo Kai Wen
www.flickr.com/yeokaiwen

The Old Iron Gate

The photo of the old iron gate embedded within the journal page is the unequivocal inspiration for this entire project. I printed the photo onto vellum paper and encased it within crackle paste to create organic substance, depth and an atmosphere of antiquity. The patina on the Wabi-Sabi tablets specifically echoes these attributes.

We are all visitors to this time, this place. We are just passing through. Our purpose here is to observe, to learn, to grow, to love—and then we return home.

—Australian Aboriginal Proverb

LIFE

The human shell withers rather expeditiously upon this terra firma. It seems just when we get the hang of living it is time to bid farewell. Life is short; therefore, wouldn't it be wise to make the most of it? What is truly important to you? What do you want to accomplish in this life? What makes you happy? Rumi gently reminds us, "Don't open the door to the study and begin reading, take down your musical instrument. Let the beauty we love be what we do. There are a hundred ways to kneel and kiss the ground." In our case, we should take down our art media and beads and begin the journey of living a rich artful existence.

Throughout this chapter I focus on some of the more challenging issues of life, the unforeseen circumstances that befall us all—sickness, spiritual angst, children leaving home and dealing with the loss of a loved one. Paramount issues such as these teach us the deepest life lessons and have a profound impact on how we perceive our purpose in this world. The depth and breadth of art journaling can take us to new levels of understanding this wild and crazy life that God has granted us.

"If you want to create, you have to sacrifice superficiality, some security, and often your desire to be liked, to draw up your most intense insights, your most far-reaching visions." *(Women Who Run with the Wolves* by Dr. Clarissa Pinkola Estés, Ph.D.). Hopefully, this authentic knowledge will spill generously into our work and fill every nook and cranny of each threaded bead.

I've been absolutely terrified every moment of my life, and I've never let it keep me from doing a single thing I wanted to do.

—Georgia O'Keeffe

LAYERS

I once wrote in an old journal, "Just below the surface lies the true me but that is by far the most difficult layer to uncover." Sometimes it is easier to explain who we are not, rather than who we are. Do you ever feel this way? I expect it is the complexity of life's layers that tend to bog us down, separating us from ourselves, sometimes to the point of obscurity. Not until we are ready to peel back these layers and uncover the place where our true being flourishes, can we truly be happy. I want to know that person; the one who is not worried about making ends meet, losing weight or raising a wise daughter; the one who has the capacity to quiet the critical voice and dissipate the irksome gloomy shadows. Perhaps we are one and the same. I am on a journey, one that does not require a plane ticket or a packed suitcase. I can reach my destination sitting in a pink, plush, velvet chair I inherited from my grandmother, from a deep swaroopa yoga pose, and especially while in the midst of taking one bead off and placing on another. Within those fleeting moments, between the inhale and the exhale, is where I believe God lives.

The Layers art journal page is a tapestry of calming elements, all of which help to restore and maintain mindfulness. I am not usually inclined to do much writing on my journal pages because I believe the pictures, colors and textures say so much more than I could ever express in words. The woodland photograph of trees appears to reflect a similar yet different image of sticks. The double illustration of the Buddha is stamped on text and tissue respectively, giving the latter a ghostly quality. The colors that fill the page originate from beautiful Zen-like art papers and fluid acrylic paints. All of the imagery is neatly packed inside a gridded landscape revealing the paradox of one who ventures to lead a balanced and spiritual life.

After the journal page was complete, I initially thought I would use painted jasper to design the necklace simply because that particular gemstone comes in such a wide variety of colors, patterns and striations. However, when I discovered glass bead artist Lori Lochner on Etsy.com, I was positive I had found the perfect set of beads for my Layers necklace. Each glass bead contained such depth and rich color. Since my journal displayed double images, I decided that my necklace should also have two striking sets of beads that complemented one another. A rough unpolished set of turquoise beads was chosen for the second strand and would make an exquisite partner.

I knew the glass beads would look wonderful strung on black leather cord. I also realized that the holes in the turquoise beads were too small to accommodate the leather cord; therefore, I needed to devise a way to complete a two-strand necklace which would accommodate two different stringing materials. Creating a double lariat knot with the leather cord and incorporating jump rings within the loops allowed me to hang the set of glass beads onto the stringing wire which held the strand of turquoise beads. Problem solving always opens the way for new designs to emmerge. I find if I ponder long enough, I usually hatch a solution, sometimes even in my sleep.

As soon as you trust yourself, you will know how to live.
—Johann Wolfgang Von Goethe

MATERIALS

(Items in **bold** are needed for the stepped-out technique)

NECKLACE

Turquoise nuggets

Green seed beads

Brown seed beads

Silver seed beads (Hill Tribe Silver)

Silver rondelles

Stamped silver rings (Hill Tribe Silver)

Primavera discs

Sterling silver "S" hook clasp

Crimp tubes

Crimp covers (optional)

Stringing wire

LARIAT

Black round leather cord, approximately 20" (51cm)

Closed jump rings, 2

Turquoise nuggets

Set of complementary glass beads (Lori Lochner Designs)

Large sterling silver pendant

TOOLS

Scissors

DOUBLE LEATHER LARIAT

Want to add quick and easy layering to a single strand necklace? Need to accommodate two different types of stringing materials in one necklace? This technique resolves these issues. Creating a double lariat and incorporating jump rings

allows you to add glass beads, pendants, charms, a small cache of expensive beads or a combination thereof to any necklace.

1. Start with a length of round leather cord cut to about 20" (51cm). Thread on a closed jump ring, positioning it about 8" (20cm) from one end. Make a small loop to secure the ring by folding over the cord. Tie a knot at the loop with the strand doubled.

2. Thread on your chosen beads, creating about a 5" (13cm) span, including a focal piece at the center. At the end of the span of beads, thread on another closed jump ring and tie another knot to secure the ring in a small loop. Try to make the knot as snug up against the beads as you can.

3. On the half of the strand that you started with, tie a knot up against the one holding the ring. Thread on a Bali spacer bead and then tie a knot after it to secure it.

STRING OF CHOICE

In this design I used round black leather cord; however, other materials such as hemp twine, silk ribbon or multiple sized stringing wire could be used instead to complement your beads of choice.

FOCUS ON YOUR FAVORITES

This particular design format is a clever solution when you only have a small number of expensive beads to use as a focal point. Complete the rest of the strand with inexpensive but good quality seed beads. Sprinkle in some silver seed beads to make it pop. From a design point of view, you can never go wrong combining leather and turquoise.

4. Snip off the excess cord at an angle, leaving about ½" (1cm) excess. Thread about four beads on the other side of the strand and tie a series of two knots to hold them on.

5. Snip the excess cord, again leaving about ½" (1cm) excess. Cut a length of beading wire to the length you want the necklace, plus about 8" (20cm). Thread a span of beads on the wire that fits between the knots of the previous strand. Thread the wire through the jump rings and then finish stringing the necklace, adding a clasp at the ends.

VISUAL MAP

If I were to visually graph the symbols for this piece, it would look something like this:

Images: *woodland photographs • moss • river • rocks • leaves • trees • Buddha • dual images*

Word combinations: *reflection • joy • life's layers*

Colors and textures: *woodland greens • earthy browns • azure • organic textures*

Mixed-media materials: *fluid acrylic paints • mica • photographs • skeleton leaves • light molding paste • crackle paste • tissue paper • transparent text • Buddha rubber stamp*

Emotions/thought process: *mindfulness • balance • peacefulness • meditation • duality • spiritual angst • ego-free life*

Beading materials/ideas: *jasper • deep green turquoise (woodland forest) • bone • copper • leather • double strands (duality)*

Layers

The woodland tapestry of calming elements restore and maintain mindfulness; however, the dual imagery demonstrates the challenge of leading an ego-free life. Color, duality and texture are pulled from the journal page and transformed into a bold jewelry design.

Trees photo by Kathy Dismus
katnap.wordpress.com

HEALING BUDDHA

I don't often have nightmares, but when I do they can surpass any *Nightmare on Elm Street* sequel. During one of my night terrors I found myself in the company of a somewhat demented nurse attempting to force my fingers—horribly deformed at the time—into a strange mechanical vise in order to straighten them. It did not take long for me to realize the symbolism in this dream. My fingers were merely a representation of the actual curvature that exists in my spine, which for most of my life has been the bane of my existence. The procedure Nurse Hatchett was diligently performing clearly corresponded to my four-hour surgery to rectify the stubborn twists and turns of a spinal column with a mind of its own—and yes, it was indeed the most agonizing experience of my life. (Hello, if this is not enough emotional substance for an art journal page then I don't know what is.)

I began to think . . . what if my back was perfect, so perfect in fact that I could expose its bare nakedness to the world without an inkling of shame? What would it be like not to worry about finding a garment that fit properly? The idea of no longer having to cloak my imperfection had the potential of producing pure joy. I could wear sundresses with spaghetti straps and a two-piece bathing suit (well, that might be taking it too far). Better still, above all else, I would be pain free. Did someone just wake me up? In reality there is no cure for what ails me; at least, that is what I have been told by several elite medical authorities (the surgery was successful only up to a certain point). Yet there are signs of hope, albeit not of the medicinal sort.

Cinematographer Conrad Hall once said, "There is a kind of beauty in imperfection," and he was absolutely correct.

Observe the kneeling woman in the art journal page hovering over water, her bare back exposed. She is enjoying the peace the stream has to offer. Perhaps she is praying or practicing a form of meditation on the Medicine Buddha. Whatever the case, something extraordinary has occurred. A butterfly rises up from the corner of the page and serves as a confirmation of her conversion. This transformation generates an innate acceptance. She acknowledges as well as embraces all of her thorns and, by doing so, is now wholly healed. I am this woman and she is me.

The creation of the Healing Buddha necklace serves as a powerful reminder of my metamorphosis by the river. Don't the slightly curved salmon colored shell beads remind you of spinal vertebrae? I purchased these shell beads long before I knew what I was going to do with them. Initially, I was intrigued by their color and texture possibilities. I pulled them out again after completing the journal page. It's amazing how this process always seems to work for me, be it on a conscious or unconscious level. Naturally, I had to include my Medicine Buddha somewhere in this necklace; hence, I decided to create a Buddha focal piece out of PMC. The grouping of the shell beads form a wavy segmented pattern which appears to imitate the curvature of the spine; consequently, symbolizing flexibility of the mind, body and spirit. Think about it; wasn't that the missing ingredient all along?

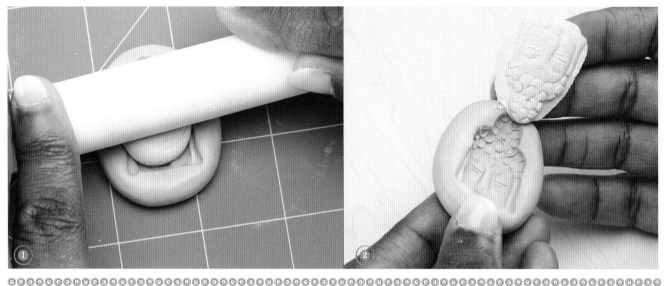

MATERIALS

(Items in **bold** are needed for the stepped-out technique)

STRAND

Stringing wire
Headpins
Shell beads
Carved bone beads
Carved bone rondelles
Large turquoise discs
Howlite discs
Wooden rondelles
Brown graduated jasper rondelles
Various African trade beads
Clasp

FOCAL PIECE

Vintage spotted wooden donut
Leather lace
Wooden rondelles
Carved bone bead
Carved bone rondelle
Silver seed beads
Silver rings
Silver round bead
Bali bead cap
Silver rondelles
Buddha charm (made from PMC)
Graduated silver disc charms (made from PMC)

CHARM
PMC
20-gauge sterling silver wire

TOOLS
PMC Tool Kit (see page 11)
Charm mold
Flush cutters
Chain-nose pliers
Round-nose pliers

PMC CHARMS

Add personal meaning to your jewelry by learning how to create charms with PMC. These tokens can mark significant milestones and act as prevailing reminders of our individual challenges and triumphs. The Buddha charm denotes healing and the set of small silver graduating discs signifies the staircase to enlightenment.

1. Take a portion of PMC+ and work it into a ball, then push it into your charm mold. I like to use a roller to work the clay into the mold.

2. Pull back the mold to release the clay.

3. Set the clay on a cutting mat and use a craft knife to trim the excess clay from around the edge.

4. To make a hole for your charm, punch a hole using a coffee stir straw.

MAKING MOLDS

Using PMC offers you the opportunity to personalize any piece of jewelry. Just purchase a desired mold or create one of your own by using a two-part silicone compound (carefully follow the manufacturer's instructions). You can make molds of intricate items such as buttons or coins. In order to replicate a three-dimensional item such as a small doll or an acorn, you would need to make a two-part mold.

5. Clean up the piece using water and a smoothing tool. If you like, stamp your initials into the back, or make any other references you like, such as a date or whatnot. Set the piece aside to dry according to the manufacturer's directions.

6. To make discs, roll your clay out fairly thin. Using clay punches, punch out five graduated circle shapes. Remove the excess clay from around the circles, using a craft knife. Using a coffee straw (or something similar), punch a hole out of the center of each disc.

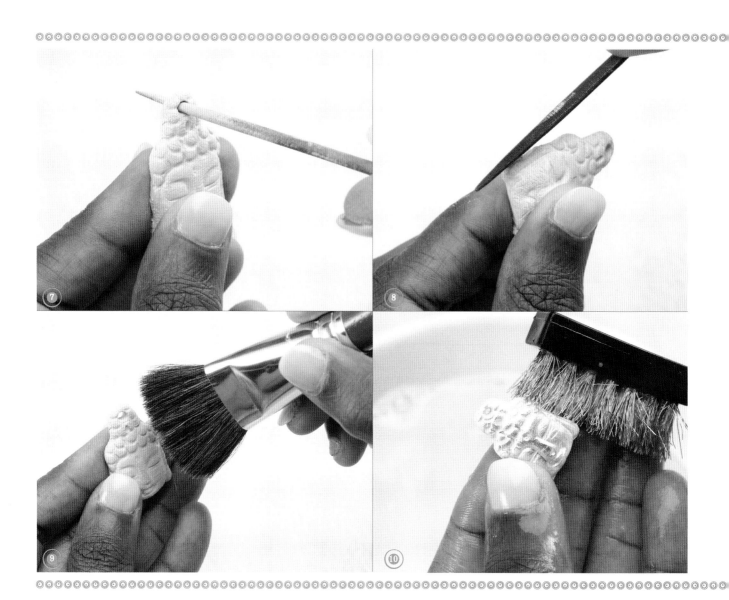

7. After it has dried for 24 hours, clean up the PMC charm by using a round file to clean up the hole area.

8. Use a flat file to clean up the seam and edges.

9. A soft brush can be used to remove the white residue.

10. Fire the charm according to the manufacturer's instruction. Once cooled, the piece can be polished using suds from dish soap and a wire brush.

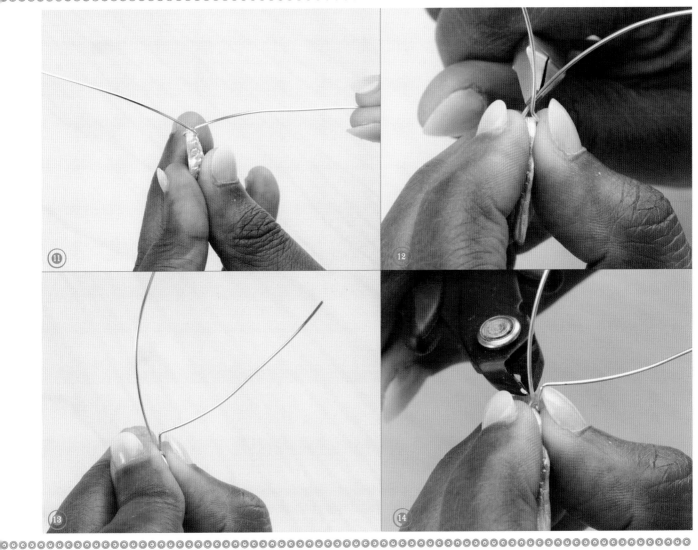

11. Cut a length of 20-gauge wire to about 6" (15cm). If your wire is tarnished, it can be cleaned up with steel wool. Thread the wire through the charm and bend each end of the wire so that they cross in the center.

12. Use chain-nose pliers to bend each wire back a bit where they cross.

13. Bend one wire down slightly so that it's at a 45-degree angle with respect to the other wire.

14. Trim the remaining wire slightly below the bent wire.

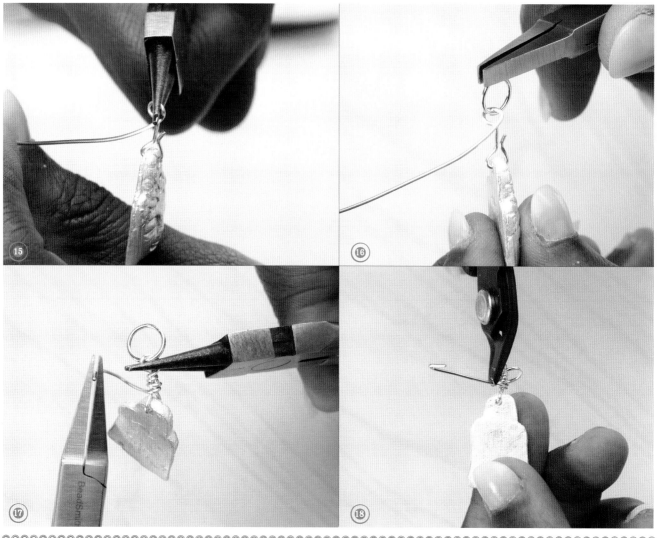

15. Grasp the loop to begin winding the
    wire around and complete the loop.

16. Thread on a jump ring.

17. Secure the loop with pliers and wrap
    the tail around the base of the loop.

18. Trim the excess wire using flush
    cutters.
    Note: See page 24 for directions on how
    to complete the centerpiece for this
    necklace, using the Knotted Leather
    Donut With Charms technique.

Alignment

Symbols such as water, nudity and a butterfly indicate change and conversion. This woman is undergoing a transformation of monumental proportions.

*Making the decision to have a child is momentous. It is to decide forever
to have your heart go walking around outside your body.*

—Elizabeth Stone

EMPTY NEST

You don't think about it when you bring the tiny bundle home from the hospital. At that moment you are lovesick, in awe of this miracle that you are solely responsible for. Then suddenly, you get it and it's enough to make you shudder due to the sheer profundity of it all. You begin to ponder all of the "firsts:" the first tooth, the first word and the first step. But the years pass quickly, and before you know it, you are schlepping through Target, helping her shop for her college gear. At some point our babies must leave home and we must learn how to cope without them.

The empty nest syndrome poses more of a threat to a single parent (or so I think because I am one). The ties that bind tend to be stronger due to years of having only each other on which to rely. Nevertheless, my only child—a daughter—is going off to college in the fall. I realize that when it is time to pack her up and take her things to the campus apartment, I won't be much good. The nerve-wracking music will no longer stream from the third floor, the cat may have some peace and there will be no need to cook every night; but still, I will dearly miss her.

Art journal pages do not always have to fit on conventional size paper. The Empty Nest page began with a narrow strip of watercolor paper. I layered the background with decorative papers, aged and waxed papers as well as text from

an old dictionary. The large focal image of the empty nest with its complicated structure accurately portrays a mother's entangled emotional state when faced with letting go and not desiring to do so.

The turquoise beads reminded me of the color of robin's eggs so I thought it fitting to include them in the design. I used only three elements in this necklace: turquoise, silver and suede, a combination that will always work well together. To bring attention to the rather ornate Bali bead, I constructed an elaborate lariat design (Infinity Twist technique) with faceted sterling silver seed beads; do not fret, it is easy to execute (see directions page 78). I also considered creating a bird's nest charm from wire and beads but dismissed this idea as too literal. Alternatively, the infinity twist configuration embodies how I will be forever intertwined and connected to my daughter long after we have both left this earth. Love is infinite; I am content in this belief.

Empty Nest

Have you ever watched a mother bird construct a nest? The meticulous way she weaves such things as twigs, leaves and other organic matter is a sight to behold. This page, along with its literal symbolism, also is an attempt at weaving assorted decorative and aged papers, waxed text and textured elements together to express the ambivalent sentiments that surface when a child is ready to leave home.

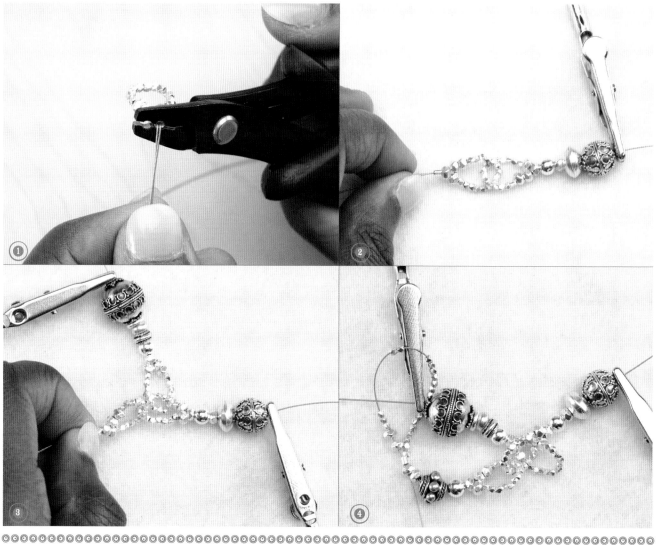

MATERIALS

(Items in **bold** are needed for the stepped-out technique)

INFINITY TWIST ELEMENT OF NECKLACE
Stringing wire
Sterling silver seed beads of varying sizes
Large ornate Bali bead
Small ornate Bali bead
Large Bali wheel spacer bead
Sterling silver saucer bead
Crimp tubes
Crimp covers

NECKLACE STRAND
Turquoise rounds
Sterling silver toggle clasp

BEAD CHARMS ON CLASP
Silver clamshell bead
Bali spacer
Turquoise round

Silver seed beads
Headpin

TASSEL
Suede lacing, 36" (91cm)
Stamped silver rings
Small silver rondelle
Stamped silver cube bead
Small silver square beads
Silver tube bead

TOOLS
Crimping pliers
Bead clip
Scissors
Tapestry needle or similar (optional)

INFINITY TWIST
This intricate-looking lariat design is easy to pull off and presents unlimited design variations.

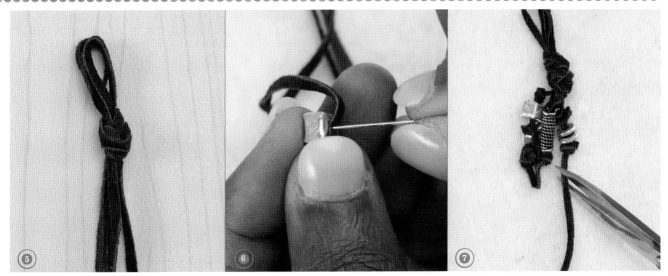

1. Cut a length of coated wire to about 12" (30cm). On one end, thread on about 15 tiny silver seed beads, a crimp tube and two larger seed beads. Thread the end of the wire through the crimp tube and the two larger beads and crimp the tube to secure the lariat loop.

2. Cover the crimp tube with a cover or, as I did, use a large-hole silver bead. Cut a new 12" (30cm) length of wire and create a second lariat in the same way, but before you thread the wire back through the beads, first thread it through the lariat from step 1. Crimp as you did before. A bead clip is handy to keep the beads on the first strand while you work on the second one.

3. Thread a couple of beads including one larger accent bead. For the final lariat, cut a new length of wire to about 10" (25cm). Create another loop on one end, threading it through the first loop, just like the last one, so that two loops are through the first one.

4. Cover the crimp tube with a cover, then thread on a Bali barrel bead, two large seed beads and then a crimp tube. Then thread on about 2" (5cm) of tiny seed beads. To create the infinity loop, run the bead-strung wire around the wire that is threaded with the large accent bead. (You will want this lariat to fit comfortably around the accent bead, so adjust the amount of seed beads

accordingly.) Then, thread the wire back through several of the tiny seed beads, crimp tube and one large seed bead. However, you do not want to run the thread through the last remaining bead before the Bali barrel bead, because it will be too difficult to crimp without proper leverage. Pull the wire taut, making sure there is no spacing between the beads. Crimp the tube bead. Trim wire. Cover the crimped bead with a crimp cover.

TASSEL

Add this quick-and-easy tassel to any piece, in the same way you would add a charm or similar dangle.

5. Cut a length of soft suede to about 36" (91cm). Fold it in half twice and tie one knot near the end with two loops.

6. Tie a second knot against the first one. Snip the loop at the other end and tie each of the four strands in a knot near the second one. Thread a bead or charm on each strand. Sometimes it's easier to get the leather through a bead or hole in a charm if you push it through with a needle or headpin.

7. Tie a second knot below each bead or charm to secure it and trim the excess suede.

WEDDING DAY

After sifting through some old photos, I found a very sweet one of my parents after they were first married. My mother told me they were out for a drive that day when they spontaneously decided to head for the shore. They stood poised, looking intently into each other's eyes. My mother's back was to the camera and I could only see my dad's face. In his eyes I saw love and sincerity of heart—he was indeed truly smitten. Although I couldn't see my mom's face, it was evident through her body language that she felt the same way. It wasn't often that I saw my parents show a public display of affection, so the photo became a significant memento of their time together. I know, without a shadow of a doubt, that my parents dearly loved one another.

I am very grateful and fortunate to have been raised by such caring, loving and supportive parents. My dad has since passed away but my mother lives close by and remains a constant anchor and close friend. My parents taught me lessons of love, loyalty, perseverance and courage—all of which I hope to pass on to my daughter as well. I can't think of anyone who deserves a journal page in their honor more than my parents.

I scanned the original photo and placed it in a file on my hard drive. Using a photo editing program on my computer I created a collage by combining several pictures, including the one of my parents at the beach. Next, I printed out a copy of the collage (applying the sepia effect to the photo) and incorporated it within the journal page. After the page was completed, I knew right away that I wanted to design a pearl necklace for my mother.

Using pearls by themselves can be very beautiful; on the other hand, if you want to "dress up" your piece even more, add antique chandelier crystals into the mix. You can often find them at garage sales (still on the original chandelier), antique stores, flea markets and secondhand shops. When I'm scouting around for vintage pieces and spot a unique crystal, I usually purchase it immediately and tuck it away for later use. Do not be concerned with the original brass findings; they can be easily removed with jewelry pliers and flush cutters. They can then be transformed into dangles using sterling silver wire (see page 54).

Attaching bead charms close together on a sterling silver link chain is an easy way to accomplish a generous clustered look, as the beads fall nicely around the neck. To add further "bling" factor, integrate marcasite beads. They are a bit pricey, but a few of them go a very long way. Marcasite beads look like sterling silver beads with inlaid crystals; in actuality, it is a mineral called white iron pyrite. Whatever the case, they are always gorgeous and come in many styles, shapes and sizes. Marcasite bead caps, rings and rondelles are also available.

MATERIALS

(Items in **bold** are needed for the stepped-out technique)

STERLING SILVER LINK CHAIN
Reclaimed antique crystal chandelier charms

White pearls

Tiny freshwater pearls

Large faux pearls

Ornate silver diamond shape beads

Bali focal bead

Marcasite focal beads

Marcasite rondelles

Marcasite bead caps

Bali bead caps

Sterling silver seed beads

Sterling silver faceted seed beads

Bali spacers

Headpins

Sterling silver clasp

TOOLS
Chain-nose pliers

Round-nose pliers

Flush cutters

MULTIPLE DANGLES ON A CHAIN
Design the ultimate charm necklace. Fashion bead dangles of various styles using pearls, marcasite beads, bead caps, rings and rondelles to hang from a link chain.

1. This necklace uses many different dangle variations, yet all are similar enough to have a cohesive look.

2. To add all the charm dangles, begin in the center of the chain with a focal element, such as this crystal.

3. For the link with the crystal, I am actually attaching a total of three dangles, using a wire wrap.

PHOTOS FOR FREE
There are several free photo editing programs which are excellent. I am currently using Picasa. This program can be downloaded from http://picasa.google.com/.

Lessons My Parents Taught Me

Old family photos have been altered with a photo editing program and then featured within the journal page in order to pay homage to loving parents.

CULTURAL CONSCIOUSNESS

It is no secret that artists such as Picasso and Matisse were greatly influenced by African art. Both were intrigued with the idea of departing from the refined European art traditions. Picasso broke new ground when he began painting the first Cubist images.

Designers have been borrowing ideas from indigenous cultures and infusing this aesthetic into all manner of construction including clothing, furniture, architecture, pottery and, in particular, jewelry, for quite some time. All one needs to do is place an online search for "ethnic jewelry" and a long list of links appears. Ethnic jewelry can be playful, simplistic, vibrant in color, grand in shape and, steeped in organic richness. With such a surplus of stimulation to choose from, is it any wonder that designers seize every opportunity to add a dose of primitive ingredients to their compositions?

In this chapter we will journey through various cultures that may potentially influence your own personal design preferences. Perhaps you will be moved to create a bit of ethnic drama in some of your own pieces.

After years of painting, drawing, sculpting or whatever, your style becomes you. You are your style. Inseparable, one and the same, no matter what you choose to create.

—Sonja Donnelly

AFRICAN WOMAN

African culture and design has had the most impact on my personal style. I like the simplicity and honesty of this stylized format. Everything about this aesthetic speaks to me on a very primal level. I am drawn to vivid color and contrast, odd accessories, chunky texture and ethnic-style beads. I thrive on juxtaposing this eclectic mixture of materials within a piece which expresses my artistic style.

How do you find your own personal style? This is a question many beginning jewelry designers ask themselves. One's design preferences and sensibilities emerge over time. Initially, you may gravitate to specific colors and materials. As your skills expand and you are able to conceptualize as well as execute more complicated techniques, your pieces will evolve and perhaps take a new direction.

In time you may recognize a visual pattern in your compositions. You will notice that you favor a specific bead shape, possess a personal color palette and select recurring icons/archetypes in your work. The day I realized that I had achieved a signature style was after receiving an email from a friend who belonged to the same online jewelry forum as

I did. It read, "I saw one of your pieces on the front page of Etsy. I recognized your style immediately!" Once you find your "inner" bead person, your designs will take off and, most importantly, express a vision that has your name written all over it.

The African Woman journal page is my interpretation of African imagery. A variety of colorful art papers and rubber stamps which project ethnic impressionism was introduced in this collage. Replicating the journal page's vibrant metaphors was accomplished by integrating African trade beads such as colorful millefiori, kakamba and inlaid bone rondelles within the design of the necklace. A tribal-like pattern of seed beads and bone rings finish off the strands. The focal ethnic pendant bead is one of many that can be found in bead stores. Other amazing materials to consider when designing ethnic jewelry include: sandcast and krobo beads, ancient shells, ostrich rings/slices, batik bone, metal artifacts, wood, coconut, horn, brass components and Coptic cross pendants. Infusing the knotted bead cluster adds an unexpected touch.

As you grow older, it dawns on you that you are yourself—that your job is not to force yourself into a style but to do what you want.

—Beth van Hoesen

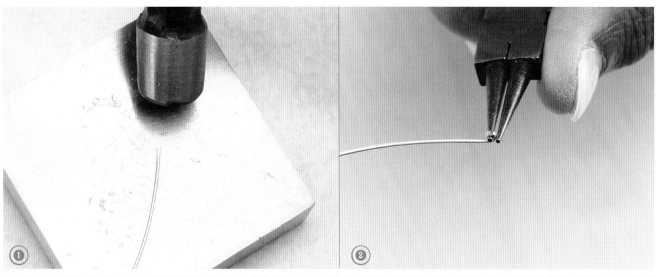

MATERIALS

(Items in **bold** are needed for the stepped-out technique)

NECKLACE

Stringing wire

Spiny orange discs

African trade beads (millefiori)

Kakamba

White howlite flat teardrop beads

Batik rings

Turquoise discs

Large wooden beads, 2

Seed beads

Small bone rings

Sterling silver toggle

Crimp tubes

Crimp covers (optional)

Large ethnic pendant

Silver seed beads

FOCAL BEAD DANGLE

Long ethnic focal bead

**20-gauge wire, 3" (8cm)
longer than your focal bead**

Wooden saucer bead

Inlaid bone rondelles

Melon bead

Kakamba bead

Coral disc

Silver bead, small

KNOTTED BEAD (BEADS FOR THIS TECHNIQUE SHOULD HAVE LARGE HOLES TO ACCOMMODATE LEATHER LACING)

Large hole focal bead

**Leather lacing, 26" (66cm) cut in half
(Silver Creek Leather)**

Large copper bead

Skunk bead (African trade bead)

Inlaid bone rondelles

Wooden saucer beads

Bone rings

Cube gems

TOOLS

Hammer

Bench block

Round-nose pliers

Flat-nose pliers

Scissors

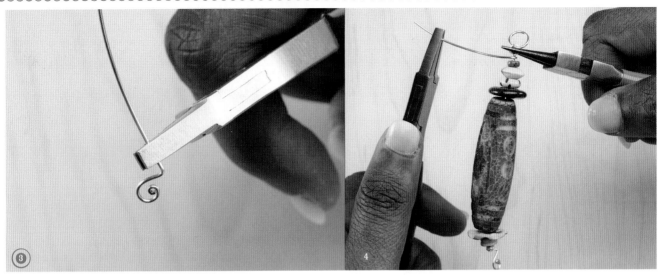

HAMMERED HEADPIN FOR FOCAL BEAD DANGLE

When you want to use a long bead (like the focal bead in this necklace), it may be difficult to find a headpin to accommodate its length. Creating your own hammered headpin allows you the freedom to use any length bead or combination of beads you desire.

1. Some long beads look nicely hung as pendants, but it can be hard to find headpins long enough to accommodate them. So make your own! Cut a length of 20-gauge wire that is approximately 3" (8cm) longer than your bead. Hammer about ¾" (19mm) of one end flat.

2. Create a tiny loop at the end, using round-nose pliers.

3. Use round-nose pliers to create a loose spiral. At the end of the spiral, make a bend in the wire using chain-nose pliers to make a small zigzag.

4. Thread beads onto your new pin and create a wrapped loop at the top to complete.

KNOTTED BEAD CLUSTER

Want to add a surprise element to any necklace? A knotted bead cluster artfully positioned on the strand of a necklace presents the designer with an opportunity to inject complementary or contrasting color and texture.

1. If you have a large-hole bead that you'd like to spruce up, you can knot some leather onto it. Start with two 13" (33cm) strands. Thread then ends of both strands through the bead.

2. Tie the two pairs of strands together into one knot.

3. Tie the entire bundle into one knot.

4. Thread one or two beads onto each individual strand, tie a knot to secure each and trim the excess.

African Woman

This page is a bold and vivid interpretation of African imagery. Most of the hues dancing harmoniously along the strand of the African Woman Necklace can trace their point of origin to this expression of cultural consciousness. The women on the page are wearing garments constructed from handmade patterns that were cut from multicolored, printed papers.

TIBETAN

One of my favorite stores to locate art papers is New York Central Art Supply located in New York City. They stock more than 6,000 types of paper from just about every part of the world. It's a collage artist's dream come true—one could simply die and go to heaven in the midst of it all! On one of my visits, I purchased several sheets of the most beautiful papers from Nepal. Some of the sheets were made translucent by an application of oil. Other papers were covered with alluring primitive block print images. To say the least, I was ecstatic to get started on an art journal page and my newly coveted papers would serve as the inspiration for a Tibetan theme.

Not only am I in love with my papers from Nepal but I am equally fascinated by actual Tibetan jewelry. The Tibetan people are deeply religious and wear their jewelry as a reminder that the truth resides within him or her. There are certain gemstones that are commonly used in making Tibetan jewelry, which include turquoise, coral, lapis lazuli and amber (my most preferred of all gemstones). I love designing with these gemstones because of their intense color, and wide range of sizes as well as cuts. In addition, I have always been intrigued with Tibetan capped beads, which brings me to my next point of inspiration.

How could I make my own capped bead without whipping out a torch and silver solder? I brainstormed several ideas and decided I could create a bead cap with leather. After a few trial-and-error attempts, I found that chamois leather worked the best due to its pliable nature. I inserted eyelets to serve as holders for bead dangles. Eyelets come in many different colors these days; therefore, you are no longer limited to just metallic choices.

Drawing inspiration from cultures throughout the world opens the door to innovative thinking and problem solving. I don't think I would have ever devised the prototype for the leather bead cap had it not been for my exposure to Tibetan jewelry.

An idea that is developed and put into action is more important than an idea that exists only as an idea.

—Buddha

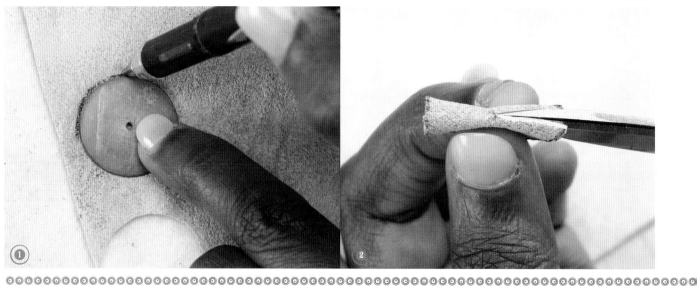

MATERIALS

(Items in **bold** are needed for the stepped-out technique)

NECKLACE STRAND

Nacozari turquoise rondelles, graduated sizes

Faceted Mexican fire opals

Faceted silver seed beads

Silver beads

Bali spacers

Bali wheel beads

Rustic sterling silver bead cap

Carnelian round

Large coral rondelles

Large turquoise discs

Large brown resin rondelles

Large resin amber barrel beads (actual amber is pricey but looks gorgeous), 2

Clasp

Crimp tubes

Crimp covers

LEATHER BEAD CAP

Chamois square, 3" x 3" (8cm x 8cm)

Pueblo Nacozari beads, 5

Mohave turquoise rondelles, 5

Faceted silver seed beads, 5

Red seed beads, 5

Headpins, 5

Brown embroidery thread

Red eyelets, 5

PENDANT

Coral round

Faceted seed bead

Bali wheel spacer bead

Large brown resin bead

Large Bali daisy spacer

Mohave rodelle

Nacozari rondelle

Jump ring

Headpin, 3" (8cm)

TOOLS

Pen

Scissors

⅛" (3mm) hole punch

Bench block

Ball-peen hammer

Eyelet setter

Embroidery needle

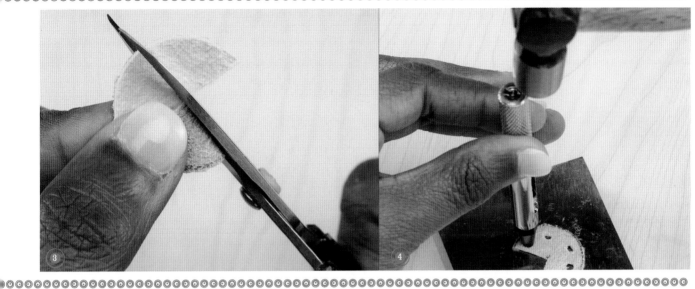

LEATHER BEAD CAP

Use this technique to accentuate a focal bead. Think of all the bead charm combinations, eyelet colors and alternate focal bead possibilities that this one technique could deliver.

1. Trace a 1" (3cm) circle onto a piece of chamois.

2. Mark a dot in the center. Cut the circle out with scissors. Fold the circle in half and cut from the outside to the center.

3. Fold the circle in the opposite direction and cut into the center again to remove a one-quarter section of the circle.

4. About ¼" (6mm) in from the outer edge, eyeball (or mark) five evenly spaced dots. Using a ⅛" (3mm) punch, punch a hole at each dot.

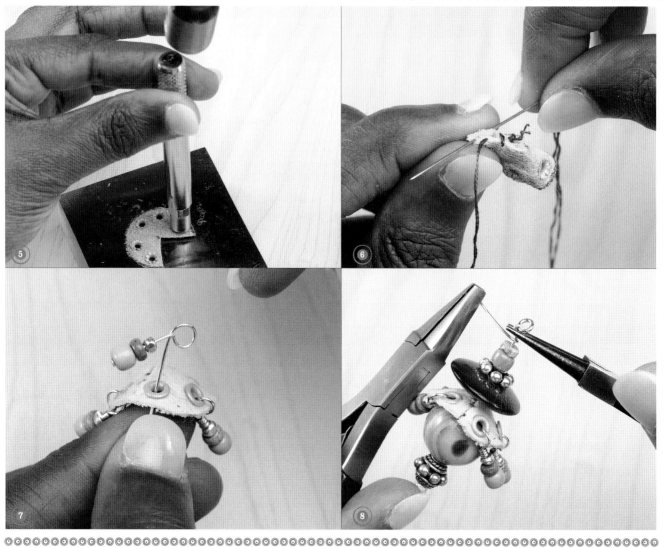

5. Set an eyelet in each hole using an eyelet setter. Insert the eyelets from the front to the back.

6. Bring the inside edges together to form a cone. Make two cross stitches using a needle and embroidery thread to hold the cone shape together.

7. From each eyelet hole, wire-wrap a bead dangle. When making loops to go through the eyelet, make them large enough to accommodate the space between the edge of the circle and the hole.

8. Create the pendant by starting with a 3" (8cm) headpin and stacking your chosen beads, which should include a large focal bead for the cap you created. Wire-wrap the threaded headpin to a closed jump ring and use the jump ring to thread onto your necklace.

Out of Tibet

The title for this page is apt, due to the fact that many of the papers that are in it actually came from Tibet. Oil-rubbed papers, authentic block prints, the image of the Buddha, as well as the turquoise painted background are all suggestive of this culture's diversity and spirit.

ABORIGINAL

Inspiration for creating can come from books of many genres, especially if they are immersed in rich and sumptuous photography. I love to glean ideas for design from books that cover topics such as art, history, decorating and culture. Books are a wonderful resource when you want to learn of another culture's perception of art—especially a society you would not have access to otherwise. Books such as *Living in China* by Taschen, *Living in Africa* by Steve Bloom and even a book on cave drawings—*Cave Art* by Phaidon, offer endless hours of eye candy and produce a flood of ideas on which to ponder. Researching the art of a specific people can open you up to even more inspiration and creativity in your own work.

Currently, one of the best books available on Aboriginal art, life and culture is *One Sun One Moon: Aboriginal Art in Australia* by Hetti Perkins, Margie West and Theresa Willsteed. Browsing through its pages and viewing the impeccable photography helps one gain an appreciation for this vital art form. Many Aboriginal artists express their paintings and jewelry by way of a predominantly earthy color palette consisting of umber, orange and ochre. The modern acrylic paintings display an unlimited range of color. The ethnic symbols, icons, graphic curves and repetitive patterns appear otherworldly and mysterious. I am deeply drawn to these images, though I am not sure why this is so.

I was not surprised to learn that creating jewelry is a traditional part of Aboriginal life. Some of their pieces are created from natural elements such as shells, seed pods, grasses, reeds, dried fruit and even snake vertebrae—any organic material that can be found in their natural environment. Items such as these symbolize their connectedness to the land. Every single component of their jewelry holds significant meaning, including the colors that are selected and in particular, the stringing material. Often someone's hair is used for this purpose, demonstrating the importance of family and community relationships. Artists paint geometric patterns, intricate dotting patterns, curved lines, concentric circles and other symbols on their beads in an effort to tell their own stories.

With this in mind, I decided to draw three beads, each designed with curved lines, patterns and symbols. I painted the beads using the predominant earthy color palette associated with Aboriginal art. Next, I attached these images within a grander landscape of color and pattern. Through these images, I tell a story, one which expresses the value and importance I place on the art of beading in my life. To further extend this process, I carefully selected a collection of ethnic beads for the Aboriginal necklace. I wanted some of the beads to be of natural materials, reminiscent of genuine Aboriginal beading practices, so I opted for beads made of seed pods, wood, leather, bone and shell. Notice how some of the beads contain concentric circle patterns, symbolic markings and vary in shape, size and color. The plethora of beads found in this necklace have been combined and configured in a multitude of styles to form a cluster of dangles that hang from a knotted leather lariat and are positioned slightly off center for added interest. The Aboriginal necklace serves as a three-dimensional manifestation of the journal page; a wearable piece of art that tells the world I am a bead artist.

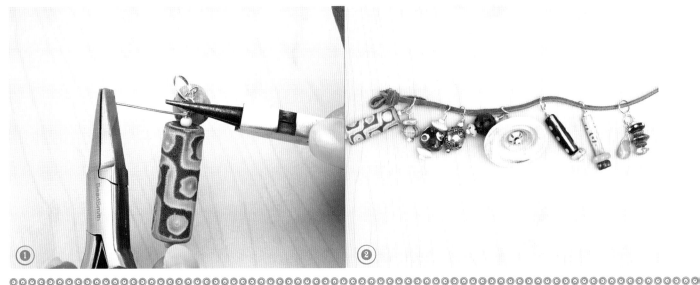

MATERIALS

(Items in **bold** are needed for the stepped-out technique)

NECKLACE STRAND

Stringing wire

Jasper rondelles

Large Carnelian round

Carnelian tooth bead

African trade bead

Copper rings

Bone rondelles

Turquoise rondelle

Clasp

Crimp tubes

Crimp covers (optional)

DANGLES ON KNOTTED LEATHER

Leather lacing, 10" (25cm)

Headpins

Leather bead

Bone batik tube bead

Bali beads

Carved bone bead

Coral rondelles

Coral rounds

Wooden saucer beads

Copper bead

African trade rondelle

Turquoise rondelles

TOOLS

Chain-nose pliers

Round-nose pliers

Scissors

DANGLES ON KNOTTED LARIAT

Add an intriguing collection of eclectic adornments consisting of color, texture and shape to any piece using this technique.

1. Create the dangles that you want to hang from the leather, including one large focal piece. Here I am going to have seven or eight. Sometimes I like to thread the jump ring from one charm onto the wire-wrapped loop of another charm before closing the loop.

2. Create a loop about 2" (5cm) from one end of the leather and tie a knot to create a closed loop. Thread your dangles onto the length of leather.

3. Pull the charms together and make a second loop at the other side of the strand of charms, then tie a knot to finish the loop.

4. Thread the loops onto your necklace strand.

VISUAL MAP

If I were to visually graph the symbols for this piece, it would look something like this:

Images: *Aboriginal symbols • turtles • snakes • beads • repetitive geometric patterns*

Word combinations: *My Story • cultural consciousness*

Colors and textures: *earthy hues • umber • beige • ochre • orange*

Mixed-media materials: *fluid acrylics • Caran d'Ache art crayons • handmade papers • ethnic patterned papers*

Emotions/thought process: *cultural awareness • primal images • connection to the land*

Beading materials/ideas: *ethnic beads • inlaid bone • shells • batik bone • leather • wood • carnelian • jasper • off-centered ethnic bead cluster*

Aboriginal Design

After being inspired by Aboriginal art through books such as *One Sun One Moon*, I rendered my interpretation of this culture's rich and soulful art form of expression.

LANTERN

Sometimes it is all about the bead, nothing but the bead . . . so help me, God. A round chartreuse vintage bead reminded me of a Chinese lantern. The color of the bead bestowed a very 1950s ambiance and was the spark that ignited a flurry of ideas for the journal page as well as the jewelry piece. The Lantern necklace is an eclectic combination of materials that took many twists and turns before it was set in stone.

There is an abundance of color going on in this piece, yet it still works. The reason it succeeds is because the entire necklace is a variation on three main colors: blue, green and pink. Once I decided to create an Asian-inspired design, it was easy locating the rest of the beads for this piece. I discovered Krystal Wick's handcrafted beads made of silk. They are gorgeous and also possess an Asian flavor that this necklace required. The enamel cloisonné bead serves as a charm hanging slightly off-center. The favored chartreuse vintage bead is placed randomly throughout the piece. The ceramic bead that serves as a focal point is adorned with knotted handcrafted silk cords. The extensions of the knot have been threaded with a farrago of beads. This is a truly funky piece that would look great with a simple white top or tank.

This is another example of a piece of jewelry actually inspiring a work of collage instead of the other way around, like most of the pieces in this book. Here, the collage was inspired by the heavy dose of pink and green and is reflected in fluid acrylics and blue paper accents. The flowers repeat the design within the cloisonné bead and the chartreuse vintage bead is echoed by the paper circles cut from green embossed art paper. The blue and white accents are lifted from the glass beads in the necklace.

It is amazing how a single bead can be the entire momentum behind your jewelry and art work.

Buddha photo by Kathy Dismus
www.katnap.wordpress.com

Lantern
Many aspects of this collage were motivated by the beads within the necklace.

MATERIALS

(Items in **bold** are needed for the stepped-out technique)

Light green pearls

Rose quartz rounds

Chartreuse vintage beads

Large white glass beads

Silver bead caps

Cloisonné bead

Turquoise round

Small stack Carico Lake turquoise chips

Pink opal briolette

Yellow opal briolette

Silver seed beads

Pink silk wrap beads (Kristal Wick)

Headpins

Toggle clasp

Focal bead

White ceramic barrel with large hole

Multicolored silk cords

Blue/white glass beads

Cloisonné rondelle

Silver spacers

Silver beads

Silver tube bead

Chartreuse vintage bead

Yellow Jade rondelle

TOOLS
Scissors

Embroidery needle

Chain-nose pliers

KNOTTED SILK CORD

Adding a knotted multicolored silk cord to a ceramic bead offers a dose of color and softness to a necklace.

1. Thread four 36" (91cm) lengths of silk cord through a large-holed bead.

2. Tie a square knot with all four strands together. (A square knot is one knot tied in one direction, followed by a second knot in the opposite direction.)

3. Tie one knot with all eight strands together.

4. Repeat with a second knot in the same direction. Push the knot up snugly against the previous knots.

5. The tying of knots from this point on is rather freeform. Each individual silk strand will get one or more beads and two or more knots. Sometimes I will tie one knot, slip on a bead, tie two more knots; sometimes I'll slip on two beads, tie one knot, slip on a third bead, tie another knot . . . and so on. When the hole in a bead is small enough to make getting the cord through it a challenge, one solution is to cut the end of the cord at a sharp angle, start it through the bead and use pliers to pull the cord out.

6. Another solution is to try gently pushing the silk through with a needle.

7. And sometimes, if the bead is exceptionally long, but the hole isn't exceptionally big, you can actually thread the needle through the cord and pull the whole needle and cord through the bead.

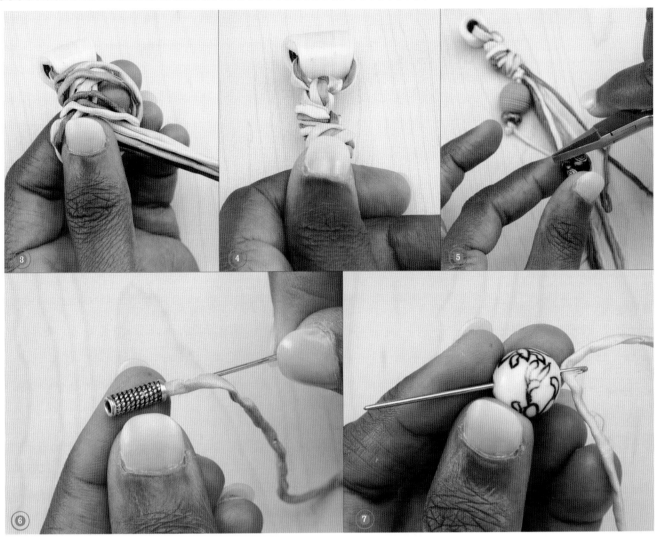

Fusion
A variation inspired by the Lantern journal page.

COLOR EXPLORATION

Every Christmas until I was eleven years old, I received a generous box of Crayola Crayons. It did not matter how many other unbelievable toys I received that day, at the end of it I was sitting quietly coloring a black-outlined Christmas tree in my annual holiday coloring book. Back then they didn't have the fancy neon, glitter or metallic variety of crayons that exist today. Had that been the case, it is certain I would have hyperventilated on the spot! Coloring was therapeutic and this small act could transport me to another place.

Color pumps through the pages of my collages and jewelry designs the same way that blood flows through my veins. It is the life force behind every brainstorm, every inspiration and, ultimately, every design. I enjoy manipulating color, painting with color, intensifying and subduing color. It is the fundamental reason why I wake up every morning.

I have included as many as twenty different colors in one piece. Why would I want to do that? Quite simply, because I can. Understanding how to properly balance color and design is essential. In this chapter we will discuss how to use color fearlessly, be it with just one color or a combination of many. There is a spirit that resides in each hue; consequently, color has the power to impact our emotions, appetite and even our sexuality. Discover how to use this property to the fullest in an effort to translate the intensity or subtlety of your current projects.

Mere color, unspoiled by meaning, and unallied with definite form,
can speak to the soul in a thousand different ways.
—Oscar Wilde

INDIGO

Who would ever think that a patch of blue could be so paramount? Blue is my favorite color. I love the calmness this color emanates, its freshness when placed next to white and the perpetual reminder of ocean and sky. Blue seems to blissfully permeate every aspect of my life, from the robin's-egg tint on my walls to my collection of blue-and-white-patterned pottery which is perched above crisp white kitchen cabinets. Like the lens on a camera, azure's magnetic power entices me to take a closer peek at a cobalt glass bottle collection resting on a lone windowsill, a strand of gorgeous faceted sapphire stones behind glass or a carton of plump blueberries at a roadside stand. It is the first color I reach for in the paint box and every single shade of this color has me equally enthralled.

One of the challenges I face as a jewelry designer is resisting the urge to use more color; therefore, working with just one color is almost impossible for me to do! I gain so much satisfaction from combining colors and visualizing contrast. However, when one comes across a strand of gemstones that not only possesses a rich natural color, a classic shape, and a near perfect cut, why add anything else to it? That is why I decided that this strand of exquisite lapis lazuli graduated rondelles would be able to go solo—well . . . almost. At times I can't even follow my own advice, which is why I had to inject just a bit of silver into this piece.

The sterling silver bead I selected has an elaborate open design to it and I wanted to take advantage of this attribute. Instead of threading the bead horizontally as expected, I changed the orientation of the bead by threading stringing wire through the area of the open design on one side of the bead. Next, I formed a lariat of silver seed beads to wrap around the bead on the opposite side (see directions page 110–112). Doing so allowed the bead to be positioned vertically as opposed to horizontally. This simple action took the design to another level and permitted me to transform this ornate focal bead into a stunning pendant. The hole that was originally intended for stringing now accommodates a headpin to which I attached a bead dangle.

The art journal page serves as a "study in blue," as I infused multiple shades of cobalt, navy, cerulean, indigo and sky within the page. I also incorporated a photograph I had taken of some of my favorite blue porcelain pieces. I urge you to try this technique when you want to play with one color or if you wish to experiment with a preferred color in combination with others. The foremost element pulled from the journal page is the river of indigo that flows seamlessly over, under and through multiple layers of collaged items. Lapis lazuli (once treasured by ancient Babylonian and Egyptian civilizations and often worn by royalty) is the only gemstone capable of capturing the richness of this blue.

Sun-bleached bones were most wonderful against the blue—that blue that will always be there as it is now after all man's destruction is finished.

—Georgia O'Keeffe

MATERIALS

(Items in **bold** are needed for the stepped-out technique)

NECKLACE STRAND

Stringing wire

Lapis lazuli graduated rondelles

Lapis lazuli rounds

Indigo blue seed beads

Faceted silver seed beads

Bali silver bead caps

Bali spacers

Silver saucer bead

Sterling silver toggle clasp

Crimp tubes

PENDANT

Large ornate sterling silver bead with an open design

2½" (6cm) 20-gauge headpins, 2

Bali spacers, 3 different styles

Silver seed beads

Jump ring

Small lapis lazuli rondelle

Small lapis lazuli round

Large lapis lazuli rondelle

Lapis lazuli disc

TOOLS

Round-nose pliers

Chain-nose pliers

Crimping pliers

ALTERED ORIENTATION FOR A BEAD

Use this technique to change the orientation of a bead that has an "open" design.

1. Thread two spacer beads onto a 3" (8cm) headpin, then insert the pin through a large decorative bead.

2. Thread on two small beads, then create a loop at the end using chain-nose pliers to first make a bend in the wire, then round-nose pliers to form the loop. Grasp the loop with the chain-nose pliers and wrap the wire around the base of the loop.

3. Trim the excess wire. Cut a 12" (30cm) length of coated wire and thread the wire through an open portion of the center of the large bead, centering it as it comes out the other side.

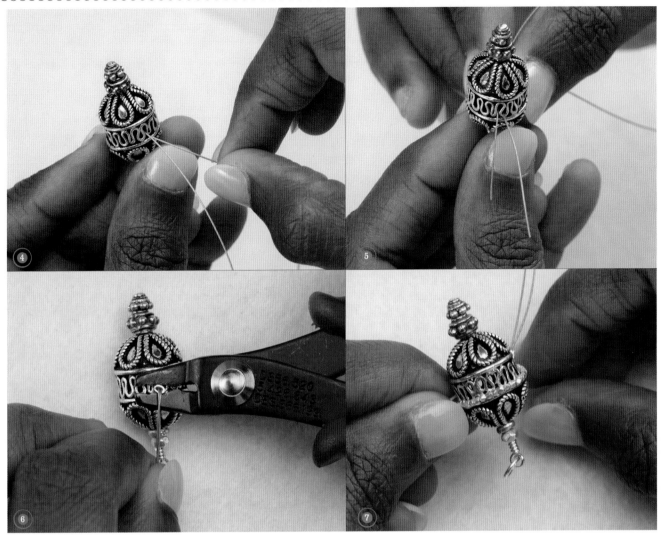

4. Insert the wire back through the same hole it came out of.

5. Maneuver the wire so that it comes out next to, but not in the same hole as the other side.

6. Add a crimp bead over both strands of the wire and crimp it next to the large bead.

7. Trim the tail (the shorter of the two) portion of the wire. Take your strand of sterling seed beads and wrap them around the center of the large bead to see approximately how many you will need.

8. Cut a new 12" (30cm) length of wire and thread the measured beads onto it as well as one large seed bead. Create a lariat by wrapping the length of beads around the large bead and securing it with a crimp bead. The wrap should be snug; you don't want the large bead to slide around.

9. Create a dangle for the bottom of the large bead by threading a small series of beads onto a 2½" (6cm) headpin.

10. Create a loop at the end of the bead stack and wrap it to the loop on the bottom of the large bead.

11. You are now ready to string the strands on either side of the large focal bead to complete the necklace.

A Study in Blue

Featuring such colors as cobalt, navy, cerulean, indigo and sky, this page serves as a study in blue. Indigo, considered one of the deepest blues, has the power to evoke a flurry of conflicting emotions which teeter on the edge of the blackest grief and, quite unexpectedly, descend gently into a pool of sweet dreams. The image of Chinese pottery, stitched patchwork, crackle-painted surfaces and the secret message of desolation, attempt to convey this color's contradictory nature.

I found I could say things with color and shapes that I couldn't say any other way . . . things I had no words for.

—*Georgia O'Keeffe*

TWO SIDES

When I was a very young child, I lived with my aunt during the week while my parents worked. Every Friday they would come to collect me and I would spend the weekends with them. I looked forward to those Fridays, anxiously awaiting their arrival, peering between the banister slats of the upstairs porch, looking for that clunky black car to cross Lee Place and land right in front of the steps. My mother's body leaned sideways, and the soft face with painted lips peeked outside the car window, our eyes met and it was as if she were looking at me for the very first time. At once I screamed her name then ferociously ran down the wooden steps into to her arms. In her hands she carried a brown paper bag and in it something special for me. What would it be today, a paint set, paper dolls or crayons and a coloring book? Either way, this is when I believe my love of color began. Even now, fifty years later, I must still have my "toys," be it pastels, paints, beads—whatever!

The journal page, Exploration of Color, is just that—an attempt to study as many colors as possible in a unique manner. The same way a writer employs a "stream-of-consciousness" to spontaneously express a mood, I proceed to randomly apply molding paste, paint, art papers and images onto paper to convey an aura of color drama. During this procedure it is important to place more emphasis on the process rather than the end product. Exploring the world of color

in this fashion is quite liberating. This same process of color exploration was repeated; however, this time with beads and with quite remarkable results. There are as many as seventeen different colors in this "Southwest"-looking necklace, many of which were plucked from the journal page. The multifarious color palette works for several reasons: a) most of the colors are a variation on the primary colors red, blue and yellow; b) silver is used as a neutral shade and helps to ground the piece; and c) the "ethnic" style of the necklace permits one to use a more liberal approach to color and design.

Using the Double Silver Seed Bead Lariat technique (pages 116–119) offers an opportunity to create the appearance of a double-strand necklace without using as many beads as you normally would for this kind of style. Also, I thought it would be nice to add a knotted Chinese coin (see page 117) as a focal conversation piece.

Exploration of Color

The artist's attempt to copiously create color drama by randomly applying molding paste, paint, art papers and images to paper. During its creation more emphasis was placed on the process rather than the product.

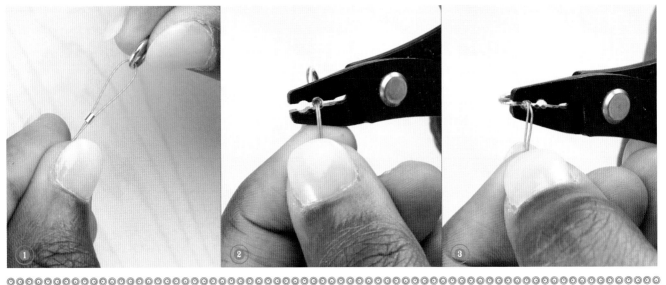

MATERIALS

(Items in **bold** are needed for the stepped-out technique)

NECKLACE STRAND

Stringing wire
Chrysoprase cube beads
Faceted sterling silver seed beads
Peruvian opal rondelle
Carved jade round
Ornate sterling silver bead
Primavera rondelles
Crimp tubes
Crimp covers
Jump rings

KNOTTED COIN PENDANT

Chinese coin
Tan leather lacing (Silver Creek Leather)
Stamped sterling silver rings
Large hole sterling silver round bead
Wooden rondelles, varying shades from dark to light
Inlaid bone saucers
Batik bone rondelles
Wooden tube bead with inlaid design
Mohave turquoise disc
Primavera discs
Turquoise rondelle
Bali spacers
Silver seed beads
Jump rings
Headpins

DOUBLE SILVER SEED BEAD LARIAT

String wire
Faceted sterling silver seed beads
Turquoise round
White vintage glass beads
Coral rounds
Lapis lazuli rondelle
Coral briolette
Thai silver heart charm
Yellow (African) turquoise rondelle
Silver spacer
Thai silver leaf charm
African trade glass bead
Crimp tubes
Crimp covers

BACK STRAND

Stringing wire
Faceted sterling silver seed beads
Bali daisy spacer
Sterling silver flower charm
Sterling silver star spacer
Sterling silver rondelles
Coral rounds
Crimp tubes
Crimp covers
Sterling silver "S" clasp

TOOLS

Crimping pliers
Chain-nose pliers
Bent chain-nose pliers
Round-nose pliers
Flush cutters

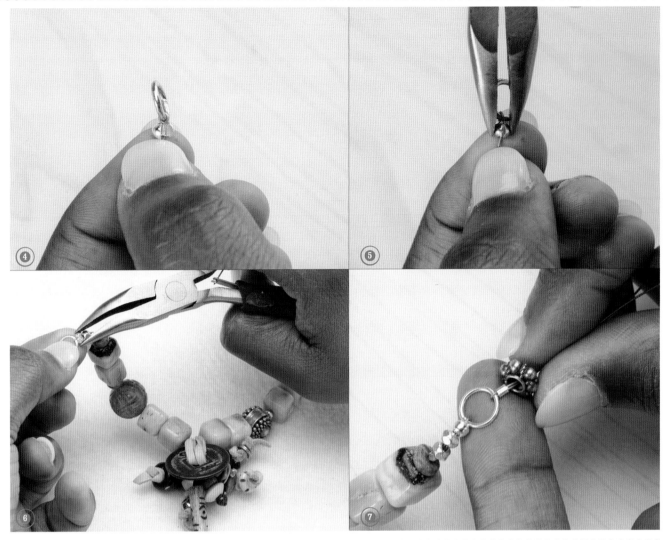

DOUBLE SILVER SEED BEAD LARIAT

This technique offers a way to create an "apron" of beads to hang from any necklace in order to convey a multi-strand appearance. In addition, this variation proposes an attractive side closure.

1. Cut a length of coated wire to about 12" (30cm). The ends of this strand are secured with crimps to a jump ring. To do this, thread on a crimp tube, thread the wire through a jump ring, then thread the wire back through the crimp tube.

2. Pull the wire taut so that the crimp tube is against the jump ring. Using the back notch of the pliers, crimp the tube with a crimper, making a U-shape. Make certain one strand is in each half of the U.

3. Squeeze the U-shape in the front notch of the pliers to collapse it onto itself.

4. Thread a crimp cover onto the opposite end of the wire and push it over the crimped tube.

5. Squeeze the cover gently to hold it in place, using bent chain-nose pliers.

6. Make a strand that includes the Knotted Leather technique (see page 24). I used a Chinese coin in lieu of the large donut bead this time. When the strand is complete, thread on another crimp tube, thread the wire through another closed jump ring, back through the crimp tube and crimp the tube just like you did on the first end. This is a little more challenging on the finished end of the strand since you are squeezing the beads close to the jump ring. (See step 8 for a helpful hint.) Finish with another crimp cover, squeezing it shut, using the bent chain-nose pliers.

7. Cut another length of coated wire to about 12" (30cm) and secure one end of it to one jump ring on the previous strand. Do this the same way you did with the crimps on the other strand, using a Bali bead spacer as the crimp cover.

8. Thread on the beads for this strand, ending with a crimp tube that is secured to a hook, in this case, a hook that came with a closed jump ring. It's easier to get the wire taut if you set one half of a pair of pliers into the loop to secure it, then pull the wire with your hands or a second plier. (Squeeze a crimp cover over the crimp tube to finish.)

9. One way to create a small cluster dangle is to wire wrap a few small beads to a piece of commercial chain. I like to work with the entire length of chain to begin with, just to make handling easier. I will trim it later. Thread three or four beads onto headpins and create a loop on each using chain- and round-nose pliers (see page 54). Thread the first bead/headpin onto the bottom link of the chain.

10. Wrap the excess length of the headpin around the base of the loop. Trim the excess headpin wire. Thread the next headpin onto the next link and wrap it to secure it as well. Skip a link and repeat for the third and fourth beads/headpins. Trim the remaining chain.

11. Set the dangle aside for a moment and begin the final strand. Start with a final length of coated wire, again about 12" (30cm). Thread a crimp tube onto one end of the wire. (See steps 2 and 3.) Next, thread on two larger seed beads, thirteen smaller seed beads and one more large seed bead. Thread the end of the wire back through the larger seed beads and the crimp tube. Pull the wire taut and crimp the tube.

12. Put a cover over the tube, or you can use a large-hole bead such as I did here. Thread on beads for the rest of your strand, including the cluster you created in steps 9 and 10. Repeat the lariat process for the end of the strand by threading on a large bead (unless you want to use a crimp cover), a crimp tube, two large seed beads, thirteen small seed beads and one final large seed bead. Again, thread the end of the wire through the large seed beads and the crimp tube (and the large-hole bead if you are using one).

13. Pull the wire taut and crimp the tube. Add a crimp cover if you didn't end with a large-holed bead. You can now thread this final strand onto the rest of the necklace. Thread one end over the hook end of that strand.

14. Thread the other end over the jump ring at the end of the first strand.

15. This necklace is meant to hook on the side.

SUNSET

Is there a special place you have visited that continues to pull at your heart long after your departure? That place for me is New Mexico. In some respects, even I find this strange, considering the fact that I spend many hours contemplating my escape to the beach. But no, it is New Mexico—the land of enchantment—which keeps calling my name. Perhaps I've lived there before in some other lifetime and my spirit still hovers longingly along the Rio Grande.

Over the course of my global travels, I have deeply appreciated seeing the Statue of David, I've gazed in awe at the Mona Lisa, and gasped—hand over chest—at the view of the Alps. I have relished a delicious alfresco meal in an Italian courtyard, admired innovative Dutch architecture and stepped inside some of the grandest cathedrals ever conceived by man. However, no place has ever moved me more than the serene blackness of a New Mexico night sky, a sunset over the Sangre de Cristo Mountains or the flora and fauna of a dusky desert landscape.

After several visits to Santa Fe, I have garnered a list of favorite haunts, specific beads stores, restaurants and galleries. However, the Georgia O'Keeffe Museum is one venue I love to revisit most. It holds more than 1,000 pieces of her work. Her art is stunning, rich in color, visually graphic and undeniably inspiring. Drawing inspiration from great artists can spur our own creativity, so it behooves us to stroll through art galleries and museums every chance we get.

The New Mexico Sojourn journal page is dedicated to my visits to New Mexico and pays special homage to Georgia O'Keeffe. Her paintbrush wonderfully captured the New Mexico landscape like no other. She enjoyed painting flowers and several of her paintings depict gorgeous deep-orange poppies. I was captivated by this warm color and decided to incorporate it into a piece of jewelry, using deep-orange faceted agate beads. Nothing expresses vibrant color more than an enameled object, but because enamel pieces can be difficult to find, I devised a plan to replicate a faux version of this art form.

Fluid acrylic paints are the perfect medium for this experiment. Using wax paper as my work surface, I began pouring small pools of different colored paints on top of each other which resulted in pleasing combinations and patterns. Once the paint "models" were dry, they resembled fired enamel. Next, I tested various resins by pouring them over each of the models to see which type worked the best. ICE Resin was the winner. It dries completely clear and serves as the perfect protective covering over the acrylic paint.

By filling bezels of countless shapes and sizes with luscious paint patterns and covering them with a protective coat of resin, one could design components such as pendants, earrings and charms. Think about the design possibilities of applying this technique! First and foremost, the color combinations are limitless. Various treatments, such as a marbled effect (see page 122), can be achieved. A layered geometric pattern could also be stunning. What about a carefully layered freeform configuration? While nothing can replace authentic enameled pieces, this technique is a quick, fun and easy alternative.

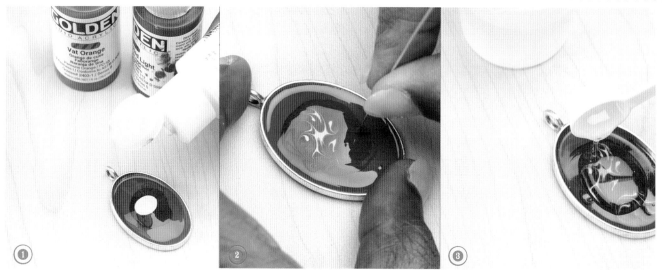

(1) (2) (3)

MATERIALS

(Items in **bold** are needed for the stepped-out technique)

Stringing wire

Faceted agate rounds

Sterling silver seed beads

Coral rounds

Coral rondelles

Black seed beads

Orange glass discs

Bali bead caps

Sterling silver toggle clasp

Crimps

Crimp covers

PENDANT

Silver oval pendant bezel (Nunn Design)

Fluid acrylic paints (Golden): Naphthol Red/Vet Orange/Titanium White

ICE Resin (Objects and Elements), including mixing cups and stir stick

PAINTED BEZEL

Create a faux enamel pendant with the vibrant colors of fluid acrylic paint and resin.

1. In a prepared bezel, squirt some fluid acrylic. Add a drop or two of two additional colors.

2. Swirl the colors around using a pin or piece of wire. Set the bezel aside to dry.

3. Mix up a small batch of resin (see pages 16–17) and pour it over your dried paint.

VISUAL MAP

If I were to visually graph the symbols for this piece, it would look something like this:

Images: *Southwest sunset • orange poppies • red chili peppers • desert images*

Word combinations: *sojourn • Land of Enchantment*

Colors and textures: *orange • umber • stucco • crackle paste*

Mixed-media materials: *fluid acrylics • resin text • resin images • oiled papers • art papers*

Emotions/thought process: *homage to Georgia O'Keeffe • spiritual home • serenity • Southwest sunset*

Beading materials/ideas: *glass discs • faceted agate • faux enamel pendant—color of sunset*

New Mexico Sojourn

Inspired by my travels throughout New Mexico, this page pays special homage to artist Georgia O'Keeffe.

RESOURCES

BEZELS

Nunn Design
www.nunndesign.com

Objects and Elements (Susan Lenart Kazmer)
www.objectsandelements.com

BEADS

Blue Healer
www.bluhealer.etsy.com
handmade glass beads

Lauri Lochner
www.lorilochner.etsy.com
handmade glass beads

Kristal Wick
www.kristalwick.com
silk fabric beads

OTHER MATERIALS

Soft Flex
www.softflexcompany.com
beading wire

Silver Creek Leather Co.
www.silvercreekleather.com
leather lacing

Levenger
www.levenger.com
Levenger Oasis Concept Pads

Objects and Elements (Susan Lenart Kazmer)
www.objectsandelements.com
ICE Resin

Golden Artist Colors, Inc.
www.goldenpaints.com
Crackle Paste

OTHER WEBSITES OF INTEREST AND INSPIRATION

PMC Guild
www.pmcguild.com

Stampington & Company
www.stampington.com

Beaducation
www.beaducation.com
online video demos and classes

INDEX

A

Aboriginal, 98–101
acrylic paint, 121
African Woman, 86–91
Alignment, 75
altered photos, 83
Ancient Voices, 22, 23, 29
art journaling, 7, 8, 19
asymmetry, 19, 21, 41, 57
Autumn, 30–33

B

balance, 19, 21
beads
    altered orientation, 109, 110–12
    capped, 93, 95–96
    double silver seed-bead lariat, 117–19
    focal, 89, 95
    knotted, 19, 20, 88, 90
    silk, 103
    wire-wrapped, 43–44
Beyond the Universe, 14, 17
bezels, 15, 35, 36, 49, 121, 122
Bliss, 14–17
blue, 108, 113
Broken Butterfly, 56

C

Cameron, Julia, 41
capped bead, 93, 95–96
chain dangles, 54
charms, 24–28, 70–74, 82
chokers, 55
cluster technique, 54
collage, 15, 35, 36, 49–50, 103
Color Exploration, 106–23
cord, knotted silk, 104
crackle paste, 29, 49–50, 61
creativity, 7, 47, 48
Cultural Consciousness, 84–105

D

dangles, 54, 100
distress ink, 36
donut bead, 24–28
double lariat technique, 66, 115, 117–19

E

Empty Nest, 76–79
enameled objects, 121, 122
Exploration of Color, 115
eyelets, 93

F

faux enamel, 122
Finding Water, 41
focal bead, 89, 95
Fusion, 105

H

headpin, 89
Healing Buddha, 68–75
holes, 59
Home, 40–45

I

I Remember Sky, 51
imperfection, 69
Indigo, 108–13
infinity twist technique, 35, 77, 78–79
inspiration, 7, 8, 26, 35, 47, 61, 99

J

Journey Back, 45
jump rings, 66

K

knotted bead, 19, 20, 53, 88, 90
knotted lariat technique, 22, 100
knotted leather donut, 24–28
knotted silk cord, 104

INDEX

L

Lantern, 102–5
Lapis Buddha, 119
lapis lazuli, 108
lariat, knotted, 22, 100
layering, 31
Layers, 64–67
leather, 20, 66, 93
Lessons My Parents Taught Me, 83
Life, 62–83
liver of sulfur, 53, 56, 57, 58, 60

M

magnification, 35
marbled effect, 121
marcasite, 81
materials, 10–11
mixed media, 7, 15
molds, 71

N

Nature's Renderings, 12–37
New Mexico Sojourn, 123

O

O'Keeffe, Georgia, 121
Old Iron Gate, 61
Organic Elements, 34–37
Out of Tibet, 97

P

paint, acrylic, 121
patina, 57, 60
personal style, 87
photos, 81, 82, 83
poetry, 15, 25
precious metal clay (PMC),
11, 56, 57, 58, 70–74

R

Reclining Woman, 53, 55
resin, 15, 35, 49, 50, 121
resin collage technique, 14, 16

S

Secret, 52–55
Sense of Place, 38–61
silk, 103, 104
Sky, 46–51
Spring, 18–21
stamps/stamping, 57, 59
steel wool, 73
Study in Blue, 113
style, personal, 87
Sunset, 120–23
supplies, 10–11

T

tarnish, 73
tassel, 79
Tibetan, 92–97
toggle, 32–33
tools, 10–11
transparencies, 19
Tree, 22–29
turquoise, 66
Two Sides, 114–19

W

Wabi-Sabi, 56–61
Wedding Day, 80–83
wire-wrapped bead, 43–44
work space, 48

June Roman embodies an odd twist of ambiguities: She loves designing jewelry although she rarely wears any; feels at ease with pen and paper yet her spelling may be suspect; and she possesses an innate talent to manipulate color in the most moving and intriguing ways even though a brief stint in a color theory class proved disastrous. Oh, and one more thing, she owns a cat named Ricko despite the fact that animals are really not her "thing."

She is a teacher, mixed-media artist, jewelry designer and writer who resides outside the Atlanta metropolitan area. She entered the worlds of jewelry design and mixed-media art relatively late in life. After years of experimenting with a farrago of art media, it wasn't until her sister introduced her to the new "hobby" of beading, that she uncovered her true calling. Shortly thereafter she began art journaling,

which fulfilled an intense desire to experiment with any manner of color and art media. The combination of jewelry design and art journaling affords her the opportunity to convey her unique creative style. June is at her finest somewhere between the midnight hour and just before sunrise, alone in her studio accompanied by a distinct collection of beads, decorative papers, paints, pastels, clay and fibers. *A String of Expression: Techniques for Transforming Art and Life Into Jewelry* is her first book. In 2007, June's jewelry was accepted into the Rhode Island School of Design Museum's Recycled Runway Fashion Show. Her work has also been published in the book, *1,000 Jewelry Inspirations* by Sandra Salamony, as well as in *Southern Distinction* and *Bell Armoire Jewelry* magazines.

Nighttime is really the best time to work. All the ideas are there to be yours because everyone else is asleep.

—*Catherine O'Hara*

INDULGE YOUR CREATIVE SIDE WITH THESE OTHER F+W MEDIA TITLES

AMULETS AND TALISMANS
Robert Dancik

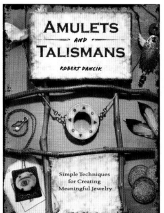

This in-depth guide is almost two books in one. Not only will you receive the guidance and insight to create jewelry that is embedded with personal meaning, but Amulets and Talismans also features extensive instruction on a wide variety of cold-connection techniques that can be applied to any style of jewelry making. Incorporate found objects, personal mementos and more into one-of-a-kind pieces of art.

ISBN-10: 1-60061-161-3
ISBN-13: 978-1-60061-161-2
flexibind with flaps • 144 pages • Z2510

A CHARMING EXCHANGE
Kelly Snelling and Ruth Rae

Inside *A Charming Exchange* you'll find the works and words of more than 30 artists with an array of varying creative styles and insights on collaborative art. Learn how to create 25 jewelry projects using a wide variety of techniques, from working with basic jewelry findings, beads and wire to incorporating mixed-media elements such as solder, fabric and found objects into charms and other jewelry projects. The book even offers ideas, inspiration and resources for you to start your own online swaps and collaborations.

ISBN-10: 1-60061-051-X
ISBN-13: 978-1-60061-051-6
paperback • 128 pages • Z1653

JOURNAL SPILLING
Diana Trout

Have you been waiting for someone to give you the right push to begin making art in your journal? Diana Trout is the good friend you've been waiting for. In the pages of *Journal Spilling* you will learn many cool new mixed-media techniques, but the biggest surprise may be what you learn about yourself. There are no lines to stay inside of here. You're free to quiet your inner critic and spill color (as well as your thoughts) all over the page. Open up and see how safe of a place your private journal can truly be.

ISBN-10: 1-60061-319-5
ISBN-13: 978-1-60061-319-7
paperback • 128 pages • Z2926

CREATIVE TIME AND SPACE
Ricë Freeman-Zachery

Discover secrets for keeping the creative part of your brain engaged throughout the day and pull yourself out of a creative rut with ideas from an insider's look into the studios of several successful artists. In her inspiring follow-up to *Living the Creative Life*, author Ricë Freeman-Zachery has gathered together a new band of artists to share their time-finding tricks and studio-savvy tips to help you find your own *Creative Time and Space*.

ISBN-10: 1-60061-322-5
ISBN-13: 978-1-60061-322-7
paperback with flaps • 144 pages • Z2953

THESE BOOKS AND OTHER FINE NORTH LIGHT TITLES ARE AVAILABLE AT YOUR LOCAL CRAFT RETAILER, BOOKSTORE OR ONLINE SUPPLIER, OR VISIT US AT WWW.MYCRAFTIVITYSTORE.COM.